WEST VANCOUVER MEMO

Withdrawn from Collection

WEDDING VOWS & TRADITIONS

WEDDING VOWS
& TRADITIONS

CATHY HOWES

MQP

MQ Publications Limited
12 The Ivories, 6–8 Northampton Street
London N1 2HY
Tel: +44 (0) 20 7359 2244
Fax: +44 (0) 20 7359 1616
email: mail@mqpublications.com
www.mqpublications.com

ISBN: 1-84072-852-3

1 3 5 7 9 0 8 6 4 2

Printed and bound in China.

Contents

WHEN IT WAS FIRST SUGGESTED THAT I SHOULD compile a book on wedding vows and traditions, I was on the verge of getting married myself so the thrill of this special occasion was at the forefront of my mind. It was at the forefront of my fiancé Ray's too, if truth be known, because he was just as enthusiastic about every element of the planning as I was, and equally enthusiastic about this book. In fact, if he had known then what he knows now, he might well have included "to love, cherish, and spend many an afternoon in libraries and dusty bookstores" in his vows! The research has been a venture that we have explored and enjoyed together and it has re-awakened an interest in poetry and philosophy which I thought I had left behind in the classroom.

Of course, every relationship is special and each has its own history, which can play a part in the proceedings in many ways. In our case, we had reunited after a 25-year gap, having been teenage sweethearts in the late 70s when hair was big and ties were even bigger! For us, the wait had been a long one but it was worth it, and we agreed that our day would be in a church—the one in which we had both been baptized—using traditional vows.

When the minister asked us beforehand what marriage meant to us, we didn't just mumble a few platitudes that we thought she wanted to hear. We went home and each wrote a mini-essay on how we felt about each other and our future. I think we were surprised at how easy it was to put feelings into words and our minister was rather impressed that we were so happy to wear our hearts on our sleeves. She was so impressed, in fact, that in place of a sermon or an address, she simply read out our words verbatim to the congregation. There wasn't a dry eye in the house!

That experience helped with *Wedding Vows & Traditions*. While we chose to recite traditional church vows, we incorporated our own feelings elsewhere in the ceremony and that is the focus of this book in many ways. If you can't— or don't want to—change the given vows of your chosen ceremony, don't automatically shy away from expressing your feelings elsewhere in the proceedings.

This book celebrates everything you might want to put into words—spoken or written—on your wedding day. It also brings together a host of time-honored traditions, so that you can learn what special customs couples from other cultures across the globe enjoy on their day. Whatever the style of your ceremony, we hope this collection of the formal and the frivolous will make you think, laugh, and above all, help you both decide how to say what you truly feel on the happiest day of your lives.

CHAPTER ONE
TIME-HONORED TRADITIONS

ALL WEDDING CEREMONIES, FROM WHATEVER FAITH or culture, are steeped in tradition, ranging from ceremonial procedure and etiquette to superstition and myth, and all have come down through the generations, over many centuries. Having a best man, for instance, is a tradition that has its origins in the olden days when a groom would quite literally steal his bride away from her hapless family. In those rough-and-ready times, the best man was the groom's co-conspirator and bodyguard. Today the best man is more likely to be the comic turn at the reception and, breaking with tradition, can sometimes even be a member of the female sex. Like many things surrounding marriage, the best "man" is a custom that has been customized.

Every culture has its superstitions too, many of which hinge on things brides and grooms should or shouldn't do on the day to ward off bad luck. The day before my own wedding, some friends asked me if I had my "something old, something new, something borrowed, and something blue." When I casually told them I wasn't bothering with all that they threw their arms in the air in horror and promptly started unclipping bracelets and searching jewelry boxes for heirlooms and baubles with a blue stone. On the morning of the big day I was offered more jewelry than I could possibly wear.

There is no escaping tradition at a wedding, especially in the wording of the vows. Couples today often get hitched (or, traditionally, plight their troth) using words and phrases that came into being hundreds of years ago, although a modernized version may be used. If you are having a religious ceremony, much of what you recite on the day will already be set out for you, although it may be possible to include some additional vows—discuss this with the member of the clergy who is to perform the wedding ceremony. It is not customary to mix traditional vows from different faiths at a religious ceremony; however, couples in a mixed faith relationship, in particular, may wish to do so.

Whether you are planning a religious or civil ceremony, there is a special charm in using vows that have echoed down the centuries, either repeating the traditional wording, or taking elements of established formats and personalizing them for a more contemporary slant. Either way, the following vows will give you some ideas. They can be used for the service itself, as part of a reading, on the invitations, or on the order of service. Perhaps these sentiments—handed from one generation to another—will help to inspire you to express everything you want to say in your own way.

I (name) take thee (name) to my wedded wife (husband),
to have and to hold from this day forward, for better for
worse, for richer for poorer, in sickness and in health, to
love and to cherish, till death us do part, according to
God's holy ordinance; and thereto I plight thee my troth.

THE BOOK OF COMMON PRAYER

＊

You have become mine for ever.
Yes, we have become partners.
I have become yours.
Hereafter, I cannot live without you.

HINDU MARRIAGE RITUAL

＊

I will be faithful to you and honest with you.

LUTHERAN WEDDING VOW

＊

I pledge, in honesty and sincerity, to be for
you a faithful and helpful husband.

TRADITIONAL MUSLIM VOW

Only about one third of weddings in Japan today are conducted in the traditional Shinto style. These ceremonies honor the kami, *the spirits of the natural world, and they are small, private affairs. Before the couple enters the room, the priest cleans and blesses the four corners of the room, and lays rice paper down on the floor. The bride and groom then come in, and sit or kneel before the priest who begins to recite prayers.*

To wed me, your promise I must be certain of, so that we may live out our lives in sweet harmony.

IRISH WEDDING VOW

✳

I take you in all love and honor, in all duty and service, in all faith and tenderness.

BASED ON TRADITIONAL PRESBYTERIAN VOWS

✳

I do solemnly declare that I know not of any lawful impediment why I (name) may not be joined in matrimony to (name).

UK CIVIL MARRIAGE CEREMONY, DECLARATORY WORDS

✳

I pledge in honesty and with sincerity to be for you an obedient and faithful wife.

TRADITIONAL MUSLIM VOW

✳

My beloved is mine and I am his.

SONG OF SONGS 2:16, THE BIBLE

Now two are becoming one,
the black night is scattered, the eastern sky grows bright.
At last the great day has come!
HAWAIIAN MARRIAGE PRAYER

❋

I will forgive you as we have been forgiven; and I will try
with you better to understand ourselves, the world, and
God; through the best and worst of what is to come,
as long as we live.
LUTHERAN WEDDING VOW

❋

To say the words "love and compassion" is easy.
But to accept that love and compassion are built upon
patience and perseverance is not easy.
TRADITIONAL BUDDHIST TEACHING

❋

Here is my hand to hold with you, to bind us for life so
that I'll grow old with you.
TRADITIONAL IRISH WEDDING VOW

*In the past, Korean grooms would
ride to their bride's home on a white pony,
bearing a white goose—a symbol of
fertility. In modern Korean weddings,
wooden geese are used. In a similar
tradition, a pair of ducks, representing the
bride and groom, are placed by the couple
in their new house: it is believed that if the
ducks face each other, then the couple is on
good terms, but if the ducks are tail to tail,
discord is in the air!*

Handfasting for a year and a day,
Bound together for a lifetime.
I will always hold your hand fast
And we shall have the time of our lives.
ADAPTED FROM THE CELTIC HANDFASTING CEREMONY

❋

I promise and covenant to be a loving, faithful and loyal
wife (husband) to you, for as long as we both shall live.
CHURCH OF SCOTLAND WEDDING VOW

❋

You are the star of each night.
You are the brightness of each morning.
You are the story of each quest.
You are the report of every land.
CELTIC SPIRITUAL BLESSING

❋

I take this ring as a sign of my love and faithfulness in
the name of the Father, the Son, and the Holy Spirit.
CHRISTIAN WEDDING VOW

Now there is no loneliness for us.
Now we are two bodies, but only one life.
APACHE INDIAN PRAYER

✳

I promise you love, honor, and respect; to be faithful to
you and not to forsake you until death do us part.
CARPATHO-RUSSIAN ORTHODOX WEDDING VOW

✳

I am the word, and you are the melody.
I am the melody, and you are the word.
TRADITIONAL HINDU MANTRA, BAHA'I FAITH

✳

We honor mother earth and ask for our marriage to be
abundant and grow stronger through the seasons.
CHEROKEE PRAYER

✳

I will share my life with you.
LUTHERAN WEDDING VOW

In early times, the handfasting ceremony signified a betrothal. The couple was betrothed for a year and a day; at the end of that time they would either choose to remain together permanently, or part without recrimination. The ceremony involved the joining of the couple's hands and an exchange of vows.

In Kashmir, the wedding couple has a special way of reciting their vows. They must stand outside, where seven one-rupee coins have been laid around a holy fire. The couple walks seven times around the fire, chanting mantras and stepping on the coins. Some Kashmiris conduct this ritual with their clothes tied together, while other Kashmiris prefer to hold hands to symbolize their union. At the end of this ceremony, the bride and groom feed each other sacred food, after which they are officially pronounced man and wife.

(Name), I take you to be my wife, to laugh with
you in joy, to grieve with you in sorrow, to grow with
you in love, serving mankind in peace and hope,
as long as we both shall live.

UNITED CHURCH WEDDING VOW

＊

May we live to grow old together in our love under our
own vine and fig tree and seeing our children's children.

ADAPTED FROM A MEDIEVAL
CHRISTIAN WEDDING CEREMONY

＊

I provide these things to my husband and home.
They are a symbol that I will care for you
and love you always.

VOW MADE DURING THE TRADITIONAL EXCHANGE OF
BASKETS AT A NATIVE AMERICAN WEDDING

＊

Let our days on the earth be long
And may we finish our roads together.

ADAPTED FROM A KERES INDIAN SONG

May our marriage last as long as it would take to place
the pieces of this smashed glass back together.

ADAPTED FROM A JEWISH WEDDING VOW

✳

We are word and meaning, united.
You are thought and I am sound.

HINDU MARRIAGE POEM

✳

The good spirits will be our cushions so that not a hair of
our heads shall be harmed.

ADAPTED FROM AN AFRICAN MARRIAGE BENEDICTION

✳

May our days be good and long upon the earth.

APACHE INDIAN PRAYER

✳

The bond that unites our hearts most perfectly is loyalty.

ADAPTED FROM THE BAHA'I WEDDING CEREMONY

At the end of a Jewish wedding ceremony, after the vows and blessings, the bride and groom share a glass of wine. The glass is then wrapped in a cloth or handkerchief and placed on the ground and the groom smashes it with his foot. All the guests then shout, "Mazel Tov" and congratulate the new husband and wife as they leave the chupah (the wedding canopy) to begin their new life together.

The custom of a bride wearing something blue at her wedding dates back many years, ever since the color blue has been thought to promote purity and fidelity. This belief has evolved from the bride's wearing a blue ribbon, through sewing a blue band around the bottom of the bride's dress, to the current trend of wearing a blue garter.

Our wedding vows are inspired by the ancient
symbol of the Golden Circle—the sacred token of
oneness, continuity, and completeness, the outward
signification of an eternal reality.

ADAPTED FROM A SPIRITUALIST WEDDING VOW

❋

We are two halves of a circle;
may the harmony of the circle be complete.

ADAPTED FROM A DRUID WEDDING CEREMONY

❋

As true lovers, once united may we show forth the
utmost faithfulness to one another.

ADAPTED FROM THE BAHA'I WEDDING CEREMONY

❋

As we light this candle, let it represent the unity of our
lives from this moment on. As this one light cannot be
divided, neither shall our lives be divided.

DRUID CANDLE-LIGHTING CEREMONY

I will be your servant, and that will console me,
for I love you dearly.

MINSTREL'S SONG, TWELFTH CENTURY

✳

Oh woman loved by me, mayst thou give
me thy heart, thy soul, and thy body.

IRISH WEDDING VOW

✳

I receive you as mine so that you become
my wife and I your husband.

CHRISTIAN MARRIAGE VOW, TWELFTH CENTURY

✳

I promise above all else to live in truth with you and
communicate fully and fearlessly.

HUMANIST PLEDGE

✳

May our trails lie straight and level before us.
Let us live to be old.

GREAT PLAINS INDIAN PRAYER

In Jewish ceremonies, vows are exchanged under a chupah *(canopy) traditionally made from the trunks of trees planted when the groom was born. The couple's respective parents escort them to the* chupah, *which is said to represent the new home the bride and groom will share in matrimony. It is open on all sides as a sign of unconditional hospitality towards friends and relatives.*

I (name) take thee (name) to be my wedded husband, to have and to hold from this day forward...to be bonny and buxom at bed and at board, to love and to cherish, till death us part, according to God's holy ordinance.

TRADITIONAL MEDIEVAL VOW

＊

I take this my friend to be my husband (wife), promising through divine assistance to be unto him (her) a loving and faithful wife (husband).

TRADITIONAL QUAKER VOW

＊

It is given that with delight and tenderness we may know each other in love.

ADAPTED FROM THE BOOK OF COMMON PRAYER

＊

I give you my hand and heart as a sanctuary of warmth and peace.

HUMANIST PLEDGE

May the joy of our bodily union strengthen the union of
our hearts and lives.

ADAPTED FROM THE BOOK OF COMMON PRAYER

✳

Father Sky and Mother Earth, creator and nurturer of
life, we give heartfelt thanks for the moment that
brought us together.

ADAPTED FROM A NATIVE AMERICAN
WEDDING BLESSING

✳

I promise to love, cherish, and protect you, whether in
good fortune or in adversity.

ADAPTED FROM A TRADITIONAL JEWISH VOW

✳

We should remember in our hearts that we will have
serious obligations to fill.

ADAPTED FROM A CHRISTIAN SERVICE,
TWELFTH CENTURY

At Hindu weddings, the "Seven Steps" are an integral part of the ceremony. In some southern Indian marriages, the couple walks towards the South while the groom holds his bride's little finger. In other parts of India, the groom holds the hand of the bride and leads her around the fire seven times. For every step taken, a blessing is chanted to bring prosperity and harmony to the newlyweds.

Our love will survive the clear light of day, continuing to
breathe life into our relationship.

ADAPTED FROM A DRUID HANDFASTING CEREMONY

＊

May the peace of the spirit be with us,
And with our children,
From the day that we have here today
To the day of the end of our lives.

ADAPTED FROM A CELTIC BLESSING

＊

May we know that riches are not needed for wealth.

ADAPTED FROM AN IRISH WEDDING SONG

＊

We shall make love often and be sensuous to one another.

ADAPTED FROM A NATIVE AMERICAN BLESSING

＊

The bond that unites our hearts most perfectly is loyalty.

ADAPTED FROM THE BAHA'I WEDDING CEREMONY

Together we will share the responsibilities of
home and children.
FIRST SAPTAPADI VOW

*

Together we will develop mental, physical,
and spiritual strength.
SECOND SAPTAPADI VOW

*

Together we will prosper and share our worldly goods.
THIRD SAPTAPADI VOW

*

Together we will fill our hearts with great joy,
peace, and happiness.
FOURTH SAPTAPADI VOW

*

Together we will raise strong and virtuous children.
FIFTH SAPTAPADI VOW

Together we will remain faithful lifelong partners.

SIXTH SAPTAPADI VOW

❉

Together we will cherish each other and our families in sorrow and happiness.

SEVENTH SAPTAPADI VOW

❉

I enter into this marriage with you knowing that the true magic of love is not to avoid changes, but to navigate them successfully.

LUTHERAN WEDDING VOW

❉

You are my husband (wife).
My feet run because of you,
My feet dance because of you,
My heart beats because of you,
My eyes see because of you,
My mind thinks because of you,
And I shall love because of you.

TRADITIONAL INUIT LOVE SONG

May the sun bring you new energy by day,
May the moon softly restore you by night,
May the rain wash away your worries
And the breeze blow new strength into your being.
May the garden of our marriage bloom with many colors,
And all the days of your life may you walk
Gently through the world and know its beauty.

ADAPTED FROM AN APACHE BLESSING

❋

Our love will survive the harsh fires of change to
continue to burn even brighter.

ADAPTED FROM A DRUID HANDFASTING CEREMONY

❋

We shall be like two sweet-singing birds perched upon
the highest branches of the tree of life, filling the air with
songs of love and rapture.

ADAPTED FROM THE BAHA'I WEDDING CEREMONY

❋

I give my body to you (name), in loyal matrimony.
And I receive it.

FRENCH CATHOLIC VOW, FIFTEENTH CENTURY

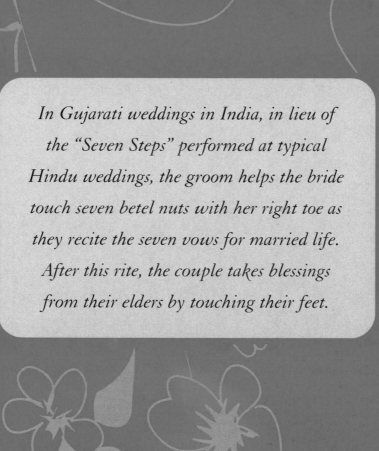

In Gujarati weddings in India, in lieu of the "Seven Steps" performed at typical Hindu weddings, the groom helps the bride touch seven betel nuts with her right toe as they recite the seven vows for married life. After this rite, the couple takes blessings from their elders by touching their feet.

This relationship is like a great tree, becoming deeper,
more rooted, and stronger with each turn of the wheel.
ADAPTED FROM THE CELTIC HANDFASTING CEREMONY

＊

We are the air. It surrounds us.
We are the fire. It burns within us.
We are the water. It flows through us.
We are the earth. It sustains us.
WICCAN HANDFASTING CEREMONY

＊

We shall be free in giving affection and warmth.
ADAPTED FROM A NATIVE AMERICAN BLESSING

＊

With this ring I thee wed, this gold and silver I thee give.
With my body I thee worship
And with this dowry I thee endow.
WEDDING VOW, TWELFTH CENTURY

As a blacksmith uses a hammer and anvil to
join two pieces of hot metal into one, so today
we forge a bond that is as strong as steel.

ADAPTED FROM AN OLD SCOTTISH CEREMONY

We shall be faithful and loyal in living our lives together.

ADAPTED FROM THE UK CIVIL MARRIAGE CEREMONY

I shall love, honor, and keep you, forsaking
all others as long as I live.

ADAPTED FROM AN EPISCOPAL WEDDING CEREMONY

May the Lord, in his goodness, strengthen our
consent and fill us with his blessings.

ADAPTED FROM A CATHOLIC VOW

I will respect, trust, help, and care for you.

LUTHERAN WEDDING VOW

For many years, the minimum legal age for marriage without parental consent was lower in Scotland than in England, so many young English couples eloped to Scotland to get married. Gretna Green was the first changing post across the Scottish border for the stagecoaches from London, and the town became a popular and convenient place to tie the knot. The "Blacksmith Priest" was often to be found officiating over an anvil. Later, in an attempt to outlaw these fleeting couples, residential restrictions were imposed which required a couple to have been living in the area for at least 21 days before they were entitled to marry. This resulted in locals taking young lovers into their homes. Finally, in 1940, Parliament ruled that marriages could only be conducted by a Minister of Religion or an authorized registrar. Gretna Green continues to attract eloping couples from all over the world.

Above us are the stars; below us are the stones
As time does pass, remember;
Like a star should our love be constant,
Like a stone should our love be firm.

ADAPTED FROM A NATIVE AMERICAN BLESSING

❋

We shall always live together in peace,
goodwill, and love.

ADAPTED FROM A CATHOLIC VOW

❋

"To everything there is a season and a time to every
purpose under the heaven." Our special time is now,
when we sow the seeds of our future together.

ADAPTED FROM ECCLESIASTES 3:1, THE BIBLE

❋

I offer you myself in marriage in accordance with the
instructions of the holy Quran.

MUSLIM VOW

We shall be close, yet not too close, possess one another,
yet be understanding. We shall be patient with each
other—storms will come, but they will go quickly.
ADAPTED FROM A NATIVE AMERICAN BLESSING

※

I pledge this sword as I pledge my soul.
Ever to be in your service.
Like this blade shall my love be strong,
Like this steel shall my love be enduring
TRADITIONAL HANDFASTING VOW

※

May I know thee more clearly, love thee more dearly,
follow thee more nearly, day by day.
BISHOP OF CHICHESTER, UK, TWELFTH CENTURY

※

When differences present themselves,
we must take counsel together,
lest we magnify a speck into a mountain.
ADAPTED FROM THE BAHA'I WEDDING CEREMONY

I knew you existed long before you understood my
desire to join my freedom to yours.

PUEBLO INDIAN VOW

※

Behold thou art consecrated unto me by this ring
according to the law of Moses and Israel.

JEWISH WEDDING VOW

※

Our love will survive the times of stillness and restriction,
continuing to anchor our hearts together.

ADAPTED FROM A DRUID HANDFASTING CEREMONY

※

As light to the eye, as bread to the hungry, as joy to the
heart, may thy presence be with me.

TRADITIONAL IRISH PRAYER

※

Our love will survive the ebb and flow of feeling,
continuing to be a well spring.

ADAPTED FROM A DRUID HANDFASTING CEREMONY

May the warmth and the light of our union be blessed.
ADAPTED FROM A DRUID CANDLE-LIGHTING CEREMONY

꙳

We are bound by the four elements; we are bound
by our love and our hearts.
WICCAN HANDFASTING VOWS

꙳

"My soul thirsteth for thee, my flesh longeth for thee in a
dry and thirsty land, where no water is." Our marriage
will be an oasis of spiritual and physical refreshment.
ADAPTED FROM PSALM 63:1, THE BIBLE

꙳

Our partnership puts love to rhyme—
Here is to loving, to romance, to us,
May we travel together without a cuss.
We alone count as none,
But together we are one.
ADAPTED FROM AN IRISH BLESSING

*At a Greek Orthodox wedding ceremony,
the bride and groom perform the "Dance of
Isaiah." They walk sedately or dance
around a central table three times, while
the best man, following behind, holds
crowns over their heads. The priest leads
the way, holding the Book of the Gospels,
from which three hymns are chanted.
The unbroken circle represents eternity and
the cross at the center represents Christ.*

In a Jewish wedding, the bride's veil is a deeply symbolic part of the ceremony. "Bedecking" involves the groom veiling his bride, and it takes place either before the ceremony or just before the couple enters the chupah. *It is thought that this ritual originates from Genesis 24:65 where Rebecca veils herself prior to her marriage to Isaac as a sign of modesty.*

I commit to you the fidelity and loyalty of my
body and my possessions.

WEDDING VOW, FOURTEENTH CENTURY

❊

Nobility of heart and memory
Combine to make me sing of goodly love;
This, let me sing, God granting me the skill
To find the words, to find the air that may
Rob slanderers of their senses, please my love,
Whom I have ever served with loyal heart
Since first I saw her, ever in my mind.

CHIVALRIC WEDDING SONG, TWELFTH CENTURY

❊

We are two bodies, but now we are breathing as one.

INSPIRED BY THE MAORI TRADITION
OF TOUCHING NOSES

❊

Love bears all things, believes all things, hopes
all things, endures all things.

I CORINTHIANS 13:4–7, THE BIBLE

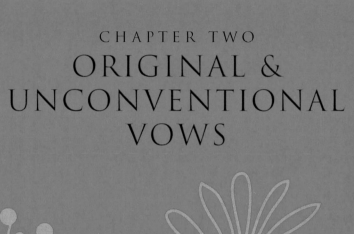

CHAPTER TWO

ORIGINAL & UNCONVENTIONAL VOWS

S OME COUPLES OBSERVE MORE WEDDING TRADITIONS and customs than others and, increasingly, the modern bride and groom are moving away from doing things the way their parents and grandparents did them. This can sometimes make waves in families, especially when the engaged couple does something that they view as "personalizing" their ceremony and it is interpreted by the older generation as being "a bit unconventional." Before anyone gets too upset however, it is worth remembering that all traditions evolve over time. The fact that we now tie an old boot to the back of the bridal car is thought to come from the days when friends and families threw their shoes after the departing newlyweds to chase off evil spirits. Even the most conservative traditionalist must recognize how that particular tradition has changed for the better!

As with every facet of a wedding, traditions become cyclical. In recent generations the large majority of weddings in the Western world have been conducted on a Saturday (apart from Jewish weddings which observe the Sabbath), putting a high market value on the most popular venues and suppliers and creating waiting lists that drag on for months or even years. Yet couples in times gone by were more flexible. They were more superstitious too, as the following rhyme reveals, but they didn't see Saturdays as written in stone.

Married on Monday, you'll have good health
Married on Tuesday, you marry for wealth
Married on Wednesday, the best day of all
Married on Thursday, the bride will know losses
Married on Friday, the bride will bear crosses
Married on Saturday for no luck at all.

As well as questioning the timing and the tone of their wedding, at many blessings and civil ceremonies couples are increasingly creating their own personalized vows, either based on traditional wording, or using totally original lines to reflect the depth of their feelings and the magnitude of the step they are taking. For some couples who are marrying for the second time, it is a way of putting the record straight or reflecting on new beginnings.

Some couples also like to inject humor and levity into the proceedings, to ensure that laughter, as well as public commitment, features strongly on the day. At a wedding where all the guests know the couple well, the vows could incorporate references to the bride and groom's history, how they met, and memorable moments in their courtship. Poetry and famous quotations or proverbs can beautifully sum up the spirit of the moment. Just remember that the wedding official needs to be kept in the picture: no surprises on the big day!

I ask you to be my wife (husband) today because nothing made real sense before I met you.

＊

You complete me. Like the final piece in a jigsaw.

＊

For love to endure it must be sure. I promise you today that I am as sure about you as I have ever been about anything.

＊

I love you truly, a little madly, but so, so deeply.

＊

I take you to be my life partner, to respect you and to love you, but also to grow with you so that we can live long and fulfilling lives together.

I want to grow old disgracefully with you!

*

As a child I was excited by the trappings of a wedding—
the white dress, the veil, the flowers, and the carriage;
As a bride I am excited by the trappings of a marriage—
the love, the support, the friendship, and you.

*

If love can be sealed with a kiss, may there be kisses
enough to make this marriage watertight.

*

I take thee to be my husband; to have and to hold and to
re-arrange your wardrobe, throw out all your decent
clothes, and buy you garish ties as presents.
SUSHMITA SEN, WWW.REDHOTCURRY.COM

*

A good marriage should be like a pot of good coffee.
Strong, energizing, and guaranteed to keep you awake
most of the night!

In Anglo-Saxon times, it was considered lucky if a couple married in a leap year, especially if the woman proposed on February 29. An old rhyme refers to this: "Happy they'll be that wed and wive, within leap year, they're sure to thrive." A Scottish document from 1288 stated that women were thereafter allowed to propose marriage to the man of their choice in a leap year. Any man who declined such a proposal had to pay a fine ranging from a kiss to payment for a silk dress or a pair of gloves.

I take thee to be my wife; to have and to hold, even though you don't understand that putting up a few shelves was not part of my engineering degree syllabus!
SUSHMITA SEN, WWW.REDHOTCURRY.COM

❋

How do you know when you have found your one true love? You don't know—you feel.

❋

I promise never to make demands on your time, I want every minute you spend with me to be given willingly.

❋

I know that we won't always agree, but I promise to respect your judgment as you have promised to respect mine.

❋

Today I pledge my body to you, in the hope that I can honor and please you and that our marriage can become richer for the intimacy we enjoy.

How long is a piece of string?
No matter, it will not stretch to match our love.

＊

Marriage is a lasting and growing love.

＊

"Cherish" is a word only ever used for the most treasured
and valued things in life. I cherish you.

＊

Wine was the nectar of the ancient gods. We drink
deeply from this cup today and pray that our life together
will always be as sweet.

＊

The most beautiful love means nothing when it is plain,
it needs engraving and silversmithing.
GUSTAVE FLAUBERT

People say that the darkest hour is that before dawn.
I will always be by your side during that hour.

✳

All opinions have value and it is the duty of us both to
remember that.

✳

Before I knew you I only lived half an existence.
Now I know I have only experienced a fraction of
the joy that is destined for us.

✳

I vow today to do everything in my power to help us
both live complete and fulfilled lives.

✳

I promise to you today a lifetime of reassurance, scattered
with more than a few pleasant surprises.

I promise today, to my one and only, that you will
be my one and only. Always.

*

To paraphrase Peter Pan, marriage has always
seemed an awfully big adventure, yet I can think of
no one better to share in the fairy tale.

*

After many dreams of how it would be,
this wedding day surpasses all fantasy.

*

You are my love and my life.

*

If I shed tears today, it will not be because of any
feelings of regret, fear, embarrassment, or awe. It will be
for the sheer thrill and emotion of marrying the most
wonderful man I have ever met.

In ancient times, the symbol of betrothal was a coin. This was broken by the young man and half of it given to his intended bride, while the other half he kept for himself. The broken coin represented his intent to return and make what is broken whole. In the Middle Ages, coins were replaced with rings. Later, in European and Middle Eastern cultures, a groom gave his bride a ring to symbolize his wealth; in Fiji, he traditionally proved he was a good catch by presenting his in-laws with a whale's tooth.

Chinese superstition decrees that it is important to marry on an auspicious day and, if possible, at an auspicious hour. The bride and groom consult a fortune-teller, who states the best day for the wedding based on their birth-dates and birth-hours. Traditionally, it was even believed that a couple should avoid marrying on the hour and marry on the half-hour instead, so that the hands of the clock were traveling upward in a positive direction, not downward in a negative one.

I pledge to you my honor, my love, and
possession of the remote control.

*

Everything I have experienced before this
day has been a rehearsal.

*

May we always appreciate each other's virtues and
forgive each other's vices. Let us promise today to help
nurture the former and overcome the latter.

*

I will surround you with my love, yet leave
you with some space.

*

I pledge to you today my love, my trust, my loyalty,
and my understanding.

I take you as my lifelong partner, friend,
lover, and soulmate.

❅

Today is more than just a party. It is a celebration of how
rewarding a life devoted to someone else can be.

❅

These vows celebrate a love that will endure
long after the confetti has been scattered and the
glasses have been drained.

❅

With the greatest joy I come into my new life with you.

❅

I promise to love and honor you but let's forget the
"obey." As an enlightened and progressive couple, we've
resolved to do everything by mutual agreement.
Haven't you darling?

This wedding ceremony cannot guarantee that our marriage will last, but my love for you can.

❋

I pledge my life and soul to you. Guard them well, as I will guard yours.

❋

Love between two people is always stronger through promise and commitment. Today I make that promise. Today I make that commitment.

❋

I love you for your beauty within.

❋

I vow to laugh at the good times and share in the sorrows—may the laughter always be loud enough to dull any pain.

May peace around this family dwell;
Make this house happy.
NAVAJO CHANT

✳

So long as we have each other's love, the rest of the
world can stay outside our door.

✳

Never again will I ask, "Who cares?"
Because now I know you do.

✳

Never doubt me.

✳

Listen to the wind…for it talks.
Listen to the silence…for it speaks.
Listen with your heart…
And you will learn and understand.
NATIVE AMERICAN BLESSING

The tradition of the bridal shower may date back to the late nineteenth century. At one gathering of a bride and her friends, a guest put a number of small gifts inside a parasol and opened it above the bride's head. Word soon spread in the fashionable press and the bridal shower was born. Another theory about the origin of this custom derives from the old tradition of the bride's father having to pay a dowry. If her father disapproved of the marriage or was too poor to provide a dowry, supportive friends and villagers offered household items as gifts.

I have no fears about entering this marriage,
and will never let the words of the unenlightened
cause me unease.

＊

We have invested in our love and our future. May our
investment always defy the law of diminishing returns.

＊

I promise never to knowingly disappoint you.

＊

May our differences be no more than minor domestic
squabbles—such as who does the dishes.

＊

Soft lips, can I tempt you to an eternity of kissing?
BEN JONSON

＊

Love makes me wise.

May we bring our own stability into an
ever-changing world.

✳

We look forward to a future of dreams,
to fulfill and share.

✳

If ever there is anything to forgive, may we find
forgiveness within.

✳

You are more precious to me than any jewel.

✳

To love a person is to agree to grow old with them.
ALBERT CAMUS

✳

Not only will I be your symbol of love, I will
be your drumkit too!

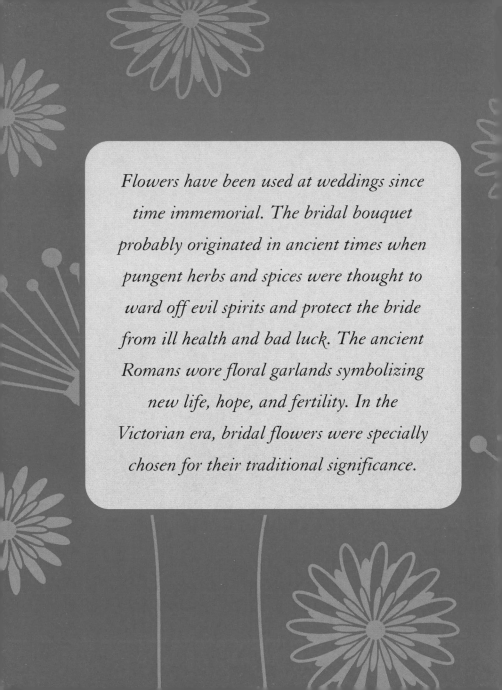

Flowers have been used at weddings since time immemorial. The bridal bouquet probably originated in ancient times when pungent herbs and spices were thought to ward off evil spirits and protect the bride from ill health and bad luck. The ancient Romans wore floral garlands symbolizing new life, hope, and fertility. In the Victorian era, bridal flowers were specially chosen for their traditional significance.

I promise to warm you when you are cold and soothe you when you are troubled.

⁂

I aspire to become the woman (man) you believe me to be.

⁂

My true love hath my heart, and I have his,
By just exchange, one for the other giv'n.
SIR PHILIP SIDNEY

⁂

No number exists that can describe the measure of my love.

⁂

I stand before you today full of trust, hope, and commitment.

A relationship built on love and honesty has the
foundations for a lifelong marriage.

✳

May our relationship be built on trust, truth,
and honesty. May we speak our minds and receive
constructive criticism in the spirit it is intended.
May we never live a lie.

✳

Totally devoted. Totally committed. Totally yours.

✳

May sincerity and fidelity be our bywords.

✳

I have for the first time found what I can truly love—
I have found you.
CHARLOTTE BRONTË

Marriage is not about meeting the right person
but being the right person.

❄

I promise to cover you with kisses.

❄

From today, let us strive to be patient and understanding,
and put each other first.

❄

I promise to be the best wife (husband) I can, so that
I am the only one you ever want.

❄

As friends and family are my witness, I vow to spend
every day of the rest of my life by your side.

❄

We make these vows in public, to keep
between ourselves in private.

We invited you here today, not to put on a show, but to show our commitment to each other.

✳

If I dismay you—tell me.
If I disappoint you—tell me.
If you love me more—tell me.

✳

Let my love, which surrounds you, fit as snugly as the ring I place on your finger.

✳

Words spoken today are only the tip of the iceberg.
True feelings beneath run even deeper.

✳

Love lies in sleep,
The happiness of healthy dreams.
JOHN CLARE

You are the core of my heart and the star of my dreams.

※

I promise that I will do my best—although it may not always seem enough!

※

A successful marriage requires falling in love many times, always with the same person.

MIGNON MCLAUGHLIN

※

It warms me, it charms me
To mention but her name:
It heats me, it beats me,
And sets me all on flame!

ROBERT BURNS

※

Every day that I wake beside you is the best day of my life.

Our love is a true love, it needs no wider recognition.

✳

Now I have made my vows, the only thing I will ever break, from this day forward, is away from the past.

✳

I ask you to support me when I waver, strengthen me when I weaken, and love me until the day we are parted.

✳

A marriage is not just a wedding, it is the joining of mind, body, spirit, and hope. Yours and mine.

✳

Take me with all my failings and faults, that we may work on them together.

✳

Promise me this—that you will always cherish me. As I promise to cherish you.

African slaves in America were forbidden from marrying. In a bid to create a new ritual to sanctify the joining of two people in symbolic, if not legal, matrimony, the practice of jumping the broom was conceived. The bride and groom took vows in the presence of a witness. A broom decorated with ribbons was jointly swept then placed on the floor to be jumped over. The broom represents several important ideas: it is, first of all, indicative of the literal and metaphorical threshold that the couple is about to cross in getting married. Moreover, starting a new life with someone requires a certain "leap of faith," symbolized by the joint leap over the broom. And finally, brooms are associated with the hearth, the center of the home.

One Navajo Indian tradition is for the couple to face East during the ceremony— the direction in which the sun rises—to represent a new beginning. Related to this tradition is the custom of the bride wearing a traditional gown with four colors: black for North, blue for South, orange for West, and white for East.

There is nothing more encouraging in life than the union of two people whose love for one another has grown through the years.

*

I promise to embrace change and grow within it.

*

I make this promise to the most important person in my life, witnessed by those dearest to me.

*

Being with you makes me want to be a better person.

*

I promise to respect your individuality and independence.

*

I do not enter into this marriage unadvisedly, lightly, or wantonly.

Today we are celebrating the mystical union of marriage.

✳

Some things were meant to be. You and I for a start.

✳

I promise to take you as my husband and partner
in all things…legal!

✳

I love you for your grace and beauty.

✳

With you I have found my home.

✳

I respect you for your integrity and judgment.

On this day, your family will become my family.

*

"Nothing lasts forever" is a sentiment for cynics.
I am an optimist and an idealist and I know that
our love will never end.

*

I am yours, you are mine—of this we can be certain.

*

Now I have your unconditional love, I know
what they've been writing about in love songs
for so many years.

*

The journey of marriage begins with the giving of
words—I give you my word.

I cherish you for your spirit.

✳

Although we already share a home, I want to take my commitment to you all the way, in front of family and friends (and God).

✳

Everything I know of you I love, but I want to know more. The lesson may take a lifetime.

✳

I vow to hold and respect your needs before my own. If you are in need of nothing, then I am satisfied.

✳

I will always carry you in my heart.

✳

I promise to keep my sense of humor when all around are losing theirs.

Irish tradition believes that it should always be a man who congratulates the bride first after the wedding ceremony, not a woman. On leaving the church, throwing an old shoe over the bride's head will bring her good luck. Later, at the reception, newlyweds are traditionally supposed to eat salt and oatmeal. If each of them eats the mixture three times, they are said to be protected against evil spirits.

There is no price on my love for you. You are more valuable and precious than any gold or jewels.

※

We all want to fall in love. Why? Because that experience makes us feel completely alive.
ANONYMOUS

※

I give you my solemn vow and promise. They may only be words, but I have never spoken words that meant so much to me.

※

I am certain that my future with you will be even better than the past we have already shared—and I can't wait to begin my new life as your wife (husband).

※

Your hopes are my hopes, and my hopes are yours. Together we can fulfill those dreams.

This is a marriage of equals.

❋

Two bodies, one heart. From today let it always
beat as one.

❋

As we light this candle together, may the flame of our
love burn brightly down the years.

❋

From this day on our lives will forever be entwined.
I vow today to always make you feel this is a bond
of love, not restriction.

❋

Marriage is a jigsaw puzzle of faith, trust, hope, and
inspiration, but the missing piece is love. Today I fit the
final piece to the puzzle.

In Swahili ceremonies, incense is burned to keep away evil spirits while the libation ceremony is performed, which is the pouring of holy water onto the floor as prayers and thanks are given to the ancestors. A Kenyan bride is bathed in sandalwood oils and henna designs are applied to her skin. A female elder, or somo, traditionally advises her on how to please her husband. She may even hide under the bridal bed in case there are any problems!

Great Spirit! Bless our children, friends, and visitors
through a happy life.

HYMN OF THE GREAT PLAINS INDIANS

❋

I vow to make your life richer, although perhaps
not your bank balance!

❋

Take me, heart, body, and soul. I give all three
willingly to you in marriage. Teach me to grow
with you every day.

❋

Soothe my troubled brow—but please don't
mess with the hair!

❋

I will always strive to illuminate your life rather
than stand in your light.

Whatever the future brings, let us promise
to never stop trying.

✳

I look at you and the whole world makes sense. With this
clarity of mind I make my pledges to you, in the
knowledge that my love for you will never change.

✳

As I make my promises today, I know that—secure in
your love—I can grow into the kind of woman you will
be proud to call your wife.

✳

If we have the solidarity and strength of the solemn vows
we make today, nothing and no one can ever shake the
foundations of our love.

✳

To know someone better is to love someone more.
Promise me that you will never let
familiarity breed contempt.

Italian brides traditionally believed wearing green the night before their wedding would bring them luck. However, in the Middle Ages, British society thought green to be a scandalous color, shown in the line of the old verse: "married in green, ashamed to be seen." In fact, to say a girl "had a green gown" implied that she was of loose morals, as her dress probably got grass stains from rolling around in fields!

*Ancient Greek weddings were known
to last three days. The bride spent the day
before her wedding with her mother and
female relatives, who gathered at the bride's
father's house to feast and make offerings to
the gods. The wedding day itself began with
a nuptial bath with spring water: the ritual
symbolized the purification of the bride
and was believed to induce fertility.
The wedding feast followed, and male and
female guests sat apart. In the evening came
the unveiling of the bride, a symbolic
moment when she was handed over to her
groom. Next came the procession from the
bride's house to her groom's, where music
and torches warded off evil spirits.
The couple spent their first night together.
The final day brought wedding
gifts and singing.*

Promise that you will always look at me the
way you do today.

I give you my solemn vow today in front of everyone
who matters most. My family, my friends, and you, the
man (woman) who completes the story of my life.

In an ideal world I have always wanted to share my life
with a charming, handsome, considerate, sensual, funny,
ingenious, kind, and considerate man. Today I step into
my ideal world (and my ideal man learns a new meaning
for the word "embarrassment").

We can promise to love, honor, and share in front of as
many witnesses as we care to invite. However, only we
know in our hearts if our pledges are true.

I will always make time for you, however late the hour.

The one true promise that any person can make is to live
a life of truth. Do you promise to build a life with me
based on trust and honesty?

※

I promise that I will try to begin every morning with
good intent and end every night without regret.

※

May I never cease to feel a thrill at saying to someone,
"have you met my husband (wife)?"

※

You're the gin in my tonic—make mine a double.

※

From this day on I look forward to exploring new ways
to cherish and love you as we enjoy the experience of
married life for the very first time.

Will you accept me and love me just as I am?
Will you roll with the mood swings and mop up the
tears? Will you laugh when I blunt your razor and tell
me I look lovely when I have gained a few pounds?
If you can accept all my faults and imperfections, you
will never find fault with my love for you.

※

If any problems should rear their ugly heads, let us vow
to fight them off first with a laugh.

※

I promise to respect you as a friend
and cosset you as a lover.
I will not promise to serve you,
because you have no need of servants.
I will not promise to obey you,
because you have no need for followers.
But I will promise to be your lover,
because everyone deserves love.

CHAPTER THREE
UNIQUE
in
EVERY WAY

EVERY WEDDING IS SPECIAL, BUT CERTAIN CIRCUMSTANCES may prompt a couple to tailor their ceremony to their own unique situation. Perhaps they are marrying their teenage sweetheart after a long separation, maybe theirs is a same-sex commitment ceremony, or maybe they are a mature couple in their golden years? With conventions being used more as a template than a strict guide today, many couples who already have children of their own or who have children from previous relationships, now invite these children to perform the roles previously played by the older generation. Some ministers and registrars will permit the bride to be escorted by her son or soon-to-be stepson rather than her father, and in many cases there is no reason why her escort need be a man at all. Many a happy bride has been escorted to her wedding ceremony by her widowed mother and there is nothing to say that this honor can't be bestowed on her daughter too if the official agrees.

These cast changes have evolved over recent generations, especially since the trend for the bride to be "given away" fell from favor among more emancipated women who preferred not to be deemed a "possession" to be passed around. Moreover, the "who gives/giveth this woman to this man?" has all but faded from many Christian ceremonies, as has the "obey" in the traditional "love, honor, and obey."

Nuptial customs handed down through the centuries can be interpreted in different ways and sometimes they are not what they might seem at first sight. A Chinese bride was traditionally carried to her wedding in a sedan chair with a sieve attached to the back, for instance, but this was less to do with her accepting the more domestic role in the household, and more to do with straining out evil. One of the best-known customs in a Jewish wedding—the groom crushing a glass underfoot—also has many explanations. For some, it symbolizes the destruction of the Holy Temple and other tragedies suffered by the Jews, and for others, it is a more positive reminder that the couple should treat their relationship with care because marriage and life are fragile, and broken shards of glass can never be put back together.

Unique circumstances involving children, second marriages, and the renewal of vows are also fertile ground for some truly moving, heartfelt sentiments. Vows can incorporate thoughts from ancient philosophers to William Shakespeare. Same-sex couples planning commitment ceremonies may find that many traditional lines can be adapted simply by removing the references to husbands and wives. From the solemn to the unconventional and lighthearted, there are lots of great ways to enter into your new life together.

FOR COUPLES WITH CHILDREN

Our family is a circle of love and strength.
With every birth and every union, the circle grows.
AUTHOR UNKNOWN

❊

We bring to this marriage our love, commitment,
and the support of our beloved children.

❊

Two's company but three (four/five) is a family.

❊

We exchange our vows today for our future
as a couple and a family.

❊

Today our family is complete. Your children are my
children, my children are your children. We are a family
drawn together by love and held together by devotion.

As your loved ones join with mine, let us go forward
together in faith and fun.

＊

We commit ourselves today to each other and
to those we love dearest.

＊

May our union be a blessing to our children.

＊

I promise to build a loyal partnership and a loving family.

＊

May our future home always ring to the sound
of love and laughter.

＊

Love me, love my family.

In Sudanese tradition, the bride and groom may bend forward and kiss the knees of their parents: this is a request for forgiveness and blessing, and it indicates the newlyweds' continued devotion to their families. This nuptial ceremony takes place beside a gargoyle flowing with water, to represent the everlasting love parents have for their children.

And we will make our wide bed beneath the bright and ragged quilt of all the yesterdays that make us who we are, the strengths and frailties we bring to this marriage—and we will be rich indeed.

AUTHOR UNKNOWN

✳

From this day forth we shall be more than one couple or two individuals—we shall be a loving and united family.

✳

The gift of children is like the gift of love—it is forever.

✳

The diversity of the family should be a cause of love and harmony, as it is in music where many different notes blend together in the making of a perfect chord.

BAHA'I SCRIPTURE

✳

Bless you all for sharing in our magical day. Today is about us, but it is something we are so proud and happy to share with you all.

Let us put our minds together and see what life we will make for our children.

SITTING BULL

✳

Now our family is complete.

✳

A husband and wife that love and value one another show their children that they should do so too.

WILLIAM PENN

✳

The center of family life is a warm and loving heart. Or even two.

✳

Let us look forward to all the friendship and happiness that comes from working and loving together as friends, lovers, and parents.

In pre-revolutionary China, wedding ceremonies were extremely elaborate. Part of the ceremony involved the groom traveling to the bride's house in a sedan chair. A quarter of a freshly slaughtered pig was placed under the bridal chair, and some firecrackers on the footstool. When the journey was complete the couple was serenaded by the exploding firecrackers. The pork was left behind, then cooked and given to beggars, a gesture which was thought to confer good fortune on the marriage.

Many years ago, brides at wedding ceremonies in Finland wore beautiful golden crowns. Nowadays, some still maintain this tradition, or they perform "The Dance of Crowns" instead. The unmarried female guests dance around the blindfolded bride and the person she puts the crown (or tiara) on will be the next woman to tie the knot.

VOWS TO INCLUDE CHILDREN

Do you (name) and (name) promise to support your
parents in their new life together?

※

I vow to cherish my parents and be a loving member of
this wonderful new family, now and always.

※

Even at your young and tender ages, do you (name) and
(name) promise to respect the institution of marriage
with as much faith as your parents here today?

※

(Name), will you promise to work together with your
parents to keep their love burning bright?

SECOND/THIRD MARRIAGE

I thank you for giving me hope and restoring
my faith in love.

*

With the strength of your love, I can turn my back on the
past and look forward to our future together.

*

Now that I have found you, I vow never to let you go.

*

I marry you with the benefit of hindsight and experience,
but with the hope and excitement of a child.

*

Thank you for teaching me to love again, for giving me
the faith to open my heart to another.

In Sudan, in a special wedding ritual, the groom stands at the entrance to his new house, while the bride stands on the inside. The equivalent of the Maid of Honor breaks an egg and the groom is pronounced master of the house. The Maid of Honor also burns and throws away seven broomsticks to symbolize the discarding of bad habits before starting a new life.

*

During a Moravian wedding, the couple lights a large candle which is passed to each guest in order for them to light their own candles. This symbolizes filling the marriage with light.

There is no blueprint for a happiness such as ours today.

※

I am prepared to learn from the past and
build on the future.

※

I waited a long time to love and be loved again.
It was worth every second.

※

The future is mapped out for us—let us enjoy the twists
and turns of the road together.

※

I come to marriage again, having known personal loss.
I am ready to bring all the positive experiences I have
gathered from that marriage to this new union.

TEENAGE SWEETHEARTS REUNITED

Today is a special day for us. Long ago you
were just a dream and a prayer.
Today we prove that dreams can come true
and prayers can be answered.

✳

You are my constant friend, my faithful partner,
my one true love.

✳

God taketh me as I am and not as I was.
Take you me so too, and let all things past pass.
JOHN HEYWOOD

✳

Our paths have crossed a thousand times before.
Thankfully we finally came to the same junction
at the same moment.

I shall love you in December with the love I gave in May.
JOHN ALEXANDER JOYCE

❄

O joy of love's awaking
Could love arise from sleep,
Forgiving our forsaking
The fields we would not reap.
ANDREW LANG

❄

I vow to love you forever, my sweetheart and soulmate.

❄

Love makes those young whom age doth chill
And who he finds young, keeps young still.
WILLIAM CARTWRIGHT

❄

Our early love was once unfinished business. Now it is
not so much finished, as about to begin anew.

Today we make the most important commitment two people can make, but I entrusted you with my heart long ago, secure in the knowledge that you would care for it.

❉

We have grown together as children and friends, let us grow old together as lovers and companions.

❉

We first met a lifetime ago and still we have a lifetime left to live.

❉

Who ever loved that loved not at first sight?
CHRISTOPHER MARLOWE

MATURE COUPLES

Two lives already richly lived, one road still to travel.
Let's not regret what might have been, but enjoy what
may unravel.

*

We make our vows today, older, wiser, but still
transfixed by the power of love.

*

Today's vows are not about the quantity but the
quality. A few years of wonderful togetherness
are better than a lifetime of second best.

*

In the fall of our lives, let us kick the leaves
hand in hand.

*

Today we invest in our future and commit to a bond
which will pay dividends and never lose interest.

We do not moan, "if only we had met earlier,"
we just give thanks that destiny finally brought us
together. Let us never waste a moment looking
back and wondering "what if?"

✳

My glass shall not persuade me I am old
So long as youth and thou are of one date.
WILLIAM SHAKESPEARE

✳

Everything that went before was only in preparation of
the happiness and fulfillment we share today.

✳

Getting married has been dubbed optimism over
experience—but who needs experience on a glorious
day such as today?

✳

Only a touch, and we combine!
ROBERT BROWNING

We pray for harmony and true happiness as we forever
grow young together.

TRADITIONAL CHEROKEE PRAYER

✳

A love worth anything is worth waiting for. Today I
pledge my love to you—you were worth the wait.

✳

Love and Time with reverence use,
Treat 'em like a parting friend
Nor the golden gifts refuse
Which in youth sincere they send:
For each year their price is more
And they less simple than before.

JOHN DRYDEN

✳

I promise to make every day count, not count every day.

✳

Anything is possible if you believe in it.

Patience is the best remedy for every trouble.
PLAUTUS

✳

Ours may be a September song, but let us sing it from
our hearts like the first day of spring.

✳

Ovid said, "Let your hook always be cast. In the pool
where you least expect it, there will be a fish." Now I can
put away my fishing rod and look for a new hobby.

✳

Lovers don't finally meet somewhere.
They are in each other's soul all along.
RUMI

✳

Bring love into your home, for this is where our
love for each other must start.
MOTHER THERESA

In a Gujarati ceremony, the groom's mother-in-law may tweak the groom's nose as he arrives, to reenact the moment when he came to the door of her house to ask for the daughter's hand. Afterwards, the bride and groom exchange garlands in the wedding hall—with this custom, they illustrate their acceptance of each other.

*

At the end of an Indian Paarsi wedding, after the vows have been exchanged, rice and rose petals are scattered over the couple. They exchange rings and the bride signs the marriage register. Finally, the bride's unmarried sister might symbolically wash the groom's feet by sprinkling them with milk.

We've been together for so long,
We behaved as if we were married.
To the world we seemed married.
But now we are married and that is the
wonderful difference.

❋

Pick the flower when it is ready to be picked.
CHINESE PROVERB

❋

Love sought is good but given unsought is better.
WILLIAM SHAKESPEARE

❋

We make these vows today in the presence of family
and friends, and surrounded by the spirits of the dear
departed. As we remember (name) and (name) in our
mind's eye, we give thanks that they were once part
of our lives and know that their spirits are with us
on this happy occasion.

RENEWAL OF VOWS

I renew my vows today, not because the earlier ones are worn, but because my love for you grows ever stronger.

✳

Our marriage is a road well traveled, and I have loved every step of the journey.

✳

It seems like only yesterday when we made our vows together. Yet time has not dulled their meaning nor diminished their value.

✳

All throughout the many years,
The smiles always outweighed the tears.

✳

Immature love says, "I love you because I need you."
Mature love says, "I need you because I love you."
CONFUCIUS

As a young woman, I stood beside you and vowed to be
your loving and faithful wife. All these years later,
I make the same promise today.

✳

Even after all these years, my heart still leaps
as you enter a room.

✳

When we are not in love too much, we are
not in love enough.

COMTE DE BUSSY-RABUTIN

✳

Thinking back to our wedding, the original
dress may not fit anymore, but my love for you
has not shrunk an inch.

✳

Ours may have been a rocky road up until now, but
we have come this far and we can travel the rest
together with confidence.

Let me not to the marriage of true minds
admit impediments.

WILLIAM SHAKESPEARE

✳

I affirm my love for you today in sight of our
family and friends.

✳

I treasure your life as if it were my own, only
more so. I would willingly give mine for you.

✳

Then you were my lover and my passion. You have
since become my best friend, too.

✳

Now we will feel no rain, for each of us
will be a shelter to the other.
Now we will feel no cold, for each of us
will be warmth to the other.

APACHE INDIAN PRAYER

I promise forever to amuse you—every great artist needs a muse.

✳

You are everything I always hoped to find in a woman (man)—all
the times I complained, I was just looking in the wrong places.

✳

If I am wrong, you always tell me.
If I am right, you always change the subject!
Don't ever change.

✳

We stand here together not to make a point.
We stand here because we are committed.
That is the point.

✳

With you by my side, I fear nothing but losing you.

✳

No walls or boundaries can keep me from your love.

CHAPTER FOUR
WITH THIS RING

ONE OF THE FOCAL POINTS OF MOST WEDDING ceremonies is the giving and exchanging of rings. For many years this was a one-way process and only the bride wore a wedding band (although quite why is not certain unless we are to suppose that men in the days of yore preferred not to advertise their married status!) It is far more likely, for the poorer members of society at least, that it was a question of cost. Gold and silver are the traditional metals of choice for a wedding, although some cultures have used baser metals, and in previous centuries a wedding band was often the biggest expense a working-class groom ever had. His fortune was, literally, tied up in the precious metal worn on his wife's finger, and it was easily portable in times of war, disease, and famine and, sadly, often a regular visitor to the pawn shop.

In days gone by, the bride's ring was also a way for a bridegroom to show that he was committed to providing for his new wife. Throughout the centuries, rings have been seen as a token of eternity but other symbols of lasting commitment were, and still are, used in some cultures today. For example, modern couples devising their own ceremonies sometimes choose an alternative token, such as a living flower, to represent this aspect of their marriage.

In the ancient classical civilizations, it was thought that an artery ran from the third finger on the left hand straight to the heart. This *vena amoris* might help explain the universal "ring finger" we still follow today. Scientific research has since proved this is not the case, but it is a charming reason to keep to the tradition.

The ring exchange during a ceremony is also a point where others in the bridal party can become involved. While it was always customary for the best man to carry the ring or rings to the ceremony, couples are increasingly looking for more innovative ways of incorporating these tokens. Some choose a ring cushion, and ask a young pageboy or bridesmaid to carry it in as part of the bridal procession, others ask the youngsters to carry the rings in a specially designed box or even on a piece of ribbon around their neck.

The way the rings get to the ceremony, however, is less important than their inclusion itself. Rings can be made from any metal and inscribed with whatever message or word the couple feels appropriate, but ultimately it is the exchange that counts, sending a loud message that the couple hopes their union will be as hardwearing as the metal and as unbroken as the circle of the ring.

I give you this ring as a sign of our marriage.

✳

I ask you to wear this ring today so that every day,
in every way, you will be carrying part of me and
my love with you.

✳

In token of our constant faith and abiding love,
I give you this ring.

✳

With this ring I thee wed, with my body I thee worship,
and with all my worldly goods I thee endow.
THE BOOK OF COMMON PRAYER

✳

I promise to care for you with love and friendship, and
to support you through good times and troubled times.
Let this ring be a sign of that promise.

Before a Swedish bride leaves for the church to be married, her mother gives her a gold coin to put in her right shoe, and her father a silver coin to put in her left. This ritual is intended to suggest that she will never go without. After the bride and groom have exchanged their vows, the new bride wears three bands on her wedding finger: one for her engagement, another for her marriage, and the third for motherhood.

This ring is for you.
You halve my sorrows and double my joys.

*

I offer you this ring as a sign of my devotion and desire
to make you happy every day for the rest of your life.

*

No material possession can ever represent the true value
of my love for you. Accept this ring as just one of the
many pledges I make today.

*

I accept this ring with the pride and passion with which
it is given. May I never give you cause to regret its gift.

*

Accept this ring today as an indication of how much
I treasure and honor you.

We exchange rings as we exchange vows, with heartfelt
sincerity, hope, and trust.

✳

By the giving and receiving of rings, we shall be known
to all as husband and wife. I accept the responsibility of
this ring as I accept the responsibility of your love. And
with all my heart I will strive to lose neither of them.

✳

Touch this ring for comfort when you are lonely;
Touch this ring for strength when you are scared;
Touch this ring and remember when we are parted;
Touch this ring and smile when you are down;
But most of all, touch this ring, as you have
touched me, with love.

✳

By accepting my love, you become my partner.
By accepting this ring, you become my wife.

In some South American countries, the groom gives his bride 13 golden coins, called arras. The coins are first blessed by the officiating priest and then passed to and from the newlyweds several times before they end up in the bride's hands. The gesture demonstrates the groom's willingness to support her in their new life together.

*

The custom of carrying the bride over the threshold may derive from an ancient Roman superstition. The Romans considered the threshold as the domain of evil spirits. If the bride were to trip up as she crossed the entrance to her new home for the first time, she may court ill fortune. Therefore the groom traditionally carried his bride over the threshold.

This ring may collect a few scratches over the years, but it will never be broken. Let it represent our future lives, held together by an unbreakable love.

*

By giving and accepting a ring, we have publicly exchanged tokens as well as promises in our ceremony today. May both be durable and everlasting.

*

Accept this simple gold band as an indication of my love—uncomplicated and neverending.

*

Accept this ring as a sign of my commitment rather than my wealth. True love has no price, but it offers infinite value.

*

In the giving and receiving of rings, we are each giving to the other a solemn promise of fidelity, loyalty, and love.

Wear this ring always and think of me. Even if we are separated by continents or oceans, I shall never be far away in spirit.

✳

I give you this ring of gold, precious and beautiful just like you, as a symbol of our union today.

✳

In token and pledge of the vow made between us, with this ring I thee wed.

✳

As we exchange rings today, so we exchange hearts, souls, and bodies.

✳

I place this ring upon your finger in the hope that every time you touch it, I will touch your heart, as you have touched mine today.

Until the sixteenth century, English customs led women to wear their wedding ring on their right hand. In 1690, however, Henry Swinburne wrote in his Treaties of Spousals, *"The finger on which the ring is to be worn is the fourth finger on the left hand, next unto the little finger; because there is a vein of blood, called* vena amoris, *which passeth from that finger to the heart." In fact, the notion of a vein running from that finger to the heart may go back as far as ancient Egypt.*

The band of gold is but an outward, public sign of a
deeply-felt personal commitment.

＊

This ring is round and hath no end.
So is my love unto my friend.

＊

Cherish this band of gold as I cherish you.

＊

I ask that you wear this ring always,
as a symbol of my love.

＊

I accept this ring as a symbol of our future journey
together—two lovers on one path.

＊

The wedding ring is the outward and visible sign of an
inward and spiritual bond that unites two loyal hearts.

I ask that you wear this ring as a constant reminder of my love for you, now and forever.

✳

Wear this ring forever as a sign of our unbroken love.

✳

This ring I give you in token and pledge of our constant faith and abiding love.

✳

These rings are not a warning to others.
They do not shout, "Keep away, we are taken."
They are a celebration, to tell the rest of the world we both love and are loved.

✳

With all that I am and all that I have, I honor you.

In the Middle Ages, if a groom could not afford a ring, he might give his bride half a broken coin and hold the other half himself. Indeed, almost all weddings, from centuries ago to the modern day, and regardless of culture or country, include an exchange of some sort of gift. The offers range from the purely symbolic, such as flowers or food, to the valuable, such as rings and money.

I accept this ring as I accept your pledge,
with gratitude and love.

*

Thank you for saying you'll have me,
Thank you for changing my life,
Thank you for being my lover,
Thank you for being my wife.

*

Wear this ring in faith and love, and with pride. It is a
symbol that says to the world, "I love and I am loved."

*

Even though your love is more precious to me than
any gold or jewel, accept this ring as a sign of our
marriage and a symbol of everlasting love.

Let these rings act as keys to unlock the
secrets of our hearts.

❋

May these rings radiate the warmth and the love
that surrounds us today.

❋

These rings are symbolic of our commitment, but your
love is the most important thing I have ever received, and
I will cherish it always.

❋

A wedding ring, like a good marriage, should be
treasured and cared for, not taken for granted and
allowed to dull.

❋

As your wedding ring wears, so will your
cares wear away.
SEVENTEENTH-CENTURY SAYING

During a Kannada Hindu wedding ceremony, the groom's wedding ring is sometimes dropped in a glass or goblet filled with colored water, and the bride and her brother play a game (called okhli*) of searching for the ring.*

*

There are several theories as to why the wedding band is worn on the third finger. One states that the third finger cannot be held out straight alone. It needs the support of the middle and little fingers either side, which gives the ring—and the union—protection.

In some West African tribal cultures, the couple exchanges rings. Gold for the husband, represents the sun in their relationship, and silver for the wife, represents the moon's influence in a woman's life. It is also customary in some African weddings for the newlyweds to exchange kola nuts. This emblem of healing illustrates that the couple will endeavor to support each other through their hardships.

You are always in my thoughts, so I offer you this ring of
faith, in the hope that I can always be in yours.

*

Let the strength of our union be as strong as this gold
and the days of our lives be as precious.

*

As gold was traditionally an indicator of wealth,
so I take this ring as a sign that our marriage will
be rich and prosperous.

*

Let these two rings, struck from the same metal,
signify two souls becoming one.

*

How do you know when a ring is a perfect fit?
It neither constricts, nor tries to escape.
How do you know when a marriage is a perfect fit?
It does the same.

May this ring be a portent of our future marriage—
strong, constant, and forever smooth.

※

This exchange of rings marks the start of a remarkable
personal journey.

※

By exchanging promises and rings, we are announcing:
"We are one in name, body, and faith."
The vows are for our families and friends today;
the rings are for the entire world.

※

These two lives are now joined in one unbroken circle.

※

Accept this ring as a symbol of my undying love. It once
graced the finger of the first important woman in my life,
my mother; now it is to be worn by the only woman
I shall ever love from this day forward, my wife.

The Maori people of New Zealand traditionally wore wedding rings made of carved bone or greenstone. The "infinity loop" has a spiritual meaning of neverending love. Some modern Maori weddings still feature a ceremonial welcome to the bride and groom and a traditional warrior challenge. The wedding ceremony is conducted by a tribal elder.

Your love illuminates my life as this golden band illuminates my hand. May neither ever lose their shine.

*

No matter what the future brings, the rings that we now exchange will be a constant reminder of the promises you have witnessed today.

*

With the giving and receiving of a ring, we are showing a public commitment to a private journey, which is represented by the unbroken circle of our wedding bands.

*

By giving me this ring, I know you are showing me your love, your passion, and your adoration. It also means you know the size of my ring finger, should you want to show me even more!

This ring, which was worn by my grandmother, represents the bond between my grandparents, which never died. May the enduring love of (name) and (name) be an example to us every day of our lives.

＊

Every time this ring glints in the sunlight, may it remind you of the one who gave it.

＊

This ring is a symbol of my love and respect for you. May it give you comfort and reassurance when we are apart and be a constant reminder of my love for you.

＊

Ever present on your finger, ever present in my heart.

＊

Accept this flower as a token of the love that will always bloom between us.

I offer you this flower as a symbol of my love,
which daily grows.

❅

Someone once said, "Life is a three-ring circus—first the
engagement ring, then the wedding ring, then the
suffering…" If today is an indication of how it feels to be
married, let us suffer together for the rest of our lives.

❅

By some standards, these rings may seem modest in
value, but their worth as symbols of our commitment
could never be equalled.

❅

No jewel—however priceless—could put a price on
our love for each other.

❅

I give you this ring, with all the love in my heart.

Although we are now bound together as man and wife,
we shall never view these rings as a bind.

*

The true value of a piece of jewelry can never be
measured by the price paid in the shop.

*

Let us sip from the same cup, to symbolize
our bond of marriage and a shared future.
BASED ON THE FRENCH TRADITION OF DRINKING
A DUAL TOAST CALLED THE *COUPE DE MARIAGE*

*

These rings mark a milestone in our journey
through life. From this day, as we wear our rings
as constant reminders of each other, we will go
forward in life together.

*

As you and I exchange rings today, let us go forth,
hand in hand, as man and wife together.

There are various theories about the origin of diamond engagement rings. Some say that the tradition started in Venice because the locals believed that marriage should be as enduring as a diamond. Others maintain that in 1477, Archduke Maximillian of Austria bought his wife-to-be, Mary of Burgundy, a vast diamond, big enough for rumors to spread and a trend for lavish and costly engagement rings to catch on. It is believed that the ancient Greeks called diamonds "teardrops of the gods," and that the gemstone's inner fire resembled the flame of everlasting love.

With the joining of hands and exchanging of rings, we
reach out to each other in a union of love, commitment,
and mutual understanding.

*

The rings so worn as you behold,
So thin, so pale, is yet of gold;
The passion such it was to prove;
Worn with life's cares, love yet was love.
GEORGE CRABBE

*

The ring is a symbol of marriage.
Smooth, unbroken, and the perfect gift
to represent the vows we have made today.

*

If marriage is the same as wedlock, this ring represents
the key that opens the lock.

*

I accept this ring, as I accept you, with love.

I give you this ring on the condition that you wear it always as a sign of my unconditional love.

✳

We have never needed jewels or trinkets to prove our love or buy affection, but I ask you to accept this ring today as the ultimate sign of my everlasting love.

✳

This ring may not be the most expensive thing I ever give you, yet it is without doubt the most precious and valuable.

✳

Let this ring represent the final step of our courtship and the first step of married life together.

✳

By accepting this ring and agreeing to become your partner for life, I reach a new level of happiness that I never thought possible.

Wedding rings have a longstanding history. In Persia, it was common practice for a bridegroom to give a ring to everyone who attended the wedding ceremony. Queen Victoria and Prince Albert even distributed six dozen rings, each engraved with the queen's profile, on the day of their wedding. Queen Victoria's engagement ring was in the form of a serpent which was believed to be a symbol of good luck.

The traditional gimmel ring was crafted to represent two hands clasped together, and came in three parts. It was often used as a betrothal token, the couple wearing one part each, the third worn by a witness or close family member. It was only finally assembled into one ring, for the bride, on the wedding day.

With all that I am and all that I have, I honor you.

＊

Tout Pour Bien Feyre (All In Good Faith).
ENGRAVED ON WEDDING BANDS IN THE MIDDLE AGES

＊

Just as our words of love are forever engraved on our
wedding rings, our feelings of love will forever be
engraved in our hearts.

＊

Despite the passing of time, may the rings we exchange
continue to radiate the same love and fortitude expressed
today until the end of our lives together.

＊

In the presence of our witnesses today, I accept this ring
as a sign of our marriage. Let everyone here assembled be
assured of our faith and devotion, and support us in our
vows, now and always.

CHAPTER FIVE

THE POWER OF LOVE

THERE ARE AS MANY SUPERSTITIONS ABOUT LOVE and courtship as there are about marriage itself. Many cultures have traditional old wives tales handed down through the centuries that promise to show eager young girls the initial of the man they will marry. In old England, it was thought that if you peeled an apple in one continuous movement and threw the complete skin into the air it would land in the shape of the letter. Another tale believed that if a girl recited the alphabet while twisting the stalk in an apple, the name of the man she was destined to marry would begin with the letter she reached when the stalk came free. And for the deeply superstitious there was also the worry of the surname. One old English rhyme warned against marrying a man with a surname that began with the same letter as the bride:

Change the name and not the letter,
Marry for worse and not for better.

Leap year also brings with it some myths and traditions. Because in most cultures it was customary for the man to propose to the woman, it became fashionable for the tables to turn and for women to pop the question in a leap year.

Opinion was divided on whether or not it was lucky to marry during this special year. The Anglo Saxons believed it was:

Happy they'll be that wed and wive
Within Leap Year they're sure to thrive.

The Greeks, however, felt differently and always believed that getting married in a leap year was a bad start to a marriage.

Remember that, ultimately, a wedding itself is all about the day—the celebration, the gathering of friends and family—but a marriage is about the rest of your life. Many couples therefore wish to include vows that express their hopes for an everlasting love. Don't hesitate to reveal the depth of your emotions—this is one occasion when you can express your feelings openly and it will be genuinely appreciated by everyone present.

When thinking about the wording of vows, you may also wish to include some thoughts on the nature of love in the order of service, readings, or wedding speeches. And if the muse is not with you when it comes to creating your own lines, there is so much beautiful prose and poetry dedicated to love that it is easy to choose pertinent words that reflect your beliefs, hopes, dreams, and intentions.

I vow today to hold you dear in my heart and work on
our partnership now and forever.

❋

I promise today to love you forever. I can promise you
this without any doubts, because until this moment
I have never truly loved.

❋

Many people search their whole life and never find that
special person. You are my special person and my life has
only just begun.

❋

I (name) take you (name) to be my wife, knowing
in my heart that you will be my constant friend and
faithful partner in life.

❋

The time we spend together is not wasted but invested.
Invested in our future and the nurture of our love.
ON A WALLED GARDEN, AUTHOR UNKNOWN

Your love fills me with a warmth and longing that
I know will comfort me for the rest of my life.

*

Til a' the seas gang dry, my dear,
And the rocks melt wi' the sun;
And I will luve thee still, my dear,
While the sands o' life shall run.
ROBERT BURNS

*

I promise to love you forever and beyond.

*

I pray that not a day goes by without us reaffirming
our love for one another.

*

I love you ever and ever and without reserve.
The more I have known you, the more have I lov'd.
JOHN KEATS

May our love grow over the years
May our lives never be blighted by tears.

✳

The future belongs to those who believe in
the beauty of their dreams.
ELEANOR ROOSEVELT

✳

May we love as long as we live, and live
as long as we love.

✳

Now that I have found you, however long "forever" is,
it will never be long enough.

✳

Today is a day you will always remember
The greatest in anyone's life.
You'll start off the day just two people in love
And end it as husband and wife.
AUTHOR UNKNOWN

In Indonesia, rice is a crucial part of the wedding feast, so a delicate pilaf colored with turmeric and enriched with coconut is traditionally served. The dish is significant because it incorporates two of the four sacred plants that Indonesian civilization is based on (rice, bamboo, banana, and coconut). Moreover, it is believed that rice is the food of fertility and yellow the color of happiness so the dish is ideal for a wedding.

Orange blossom is, in many cultures, a traditional feature of wedding ceremonies. This custom probably originated in ancient China where orange blossom was an emblem of innocence and chastity. It is one of the few plants that blooms and bears fruit simultaneously, and it is therefore associated with fertility. In Spain, France, and Greece the flowers are used in wedding ceremonies as a symbol of good fortune, chastity, innocence, or purity. In Mexico, a garland of orange blossoms is placed in a figure of eight around the necks of the couple as a sign of unity.

May the deep love that we feel for each other embrace
all those present here today.

Today I make my pledge to my friend, confidante,
partner, and lover. All of whom I love passionately.

In the spring of love comes discovery,
In the summer of love comes strength,
In the fall of love comes contentment,
In the winter of love comes parting and sorrow.
BASED ON MEDIEVAL CELTIC RITES

Grow old along with me
The best is yet to be.
ROBERT BROWNING

A new friend is like new wine; when it has aged,
you can drink it with pleasure.
AUTHOR UNKNOWN

You are more beautiful and precious to me than life itself.
I am honored that you have agreed to be mine forever.

✳

Love freely given has no beginning and no end.

✳

Before these witnesses I vow to love you and care
for you for as long as we both shall live.

✳

That this peace may last for ever,
And our hands be clasped more closely
And our hearts be more united.
HENRY WADSWORTH LONGFELLOW

✳

As the years roll by, may our looks only fade at
the same rate as our eyesight!

During ancient Greek wedding ceremonies, guests would throw fruit and flowers at the couple on their procession, perhaps as a symbolic wish for their union to be fruitful. In modern Greek weddings, the bride has been known to throw a pomegranate instead of the traditional bouquet as the seeds of this fruit are associated with fertility.

*

In Russia, the bride and groom receive bread and salt during a civil marriage ceremony to symbolize health, prosperity, and long life. The groom must then drink a shot glass of straight vodka and throw the empty glass over his right shoulder.

Our unique love cannot be defined (by society or law) but
we both understand its meaning.

✳

You and I have so much love
That it burns like a fire,
In which we bake a lump of clay
Molded into a figure of you and a figure of me.
KUAN TAO-SHENG

✳

Our future together can be whatever we want it to be, we
alone are responsible for our happiness.

✳

When we enjoy success, it will be a joint achievement.
When we experience failure, we must face it together.

✳

Let us bind ourselves together so tightly today that even
after a lifetime together, the ties will not come loose.

Serendipity brought us together, but it will be a shared faith and commitment that will keep us there.

❋

I cannot promise what the future will bring, all I know is that you will be part of it.

❋

We thank our married friends and family for the examples they have shown us and vow to follow in their footsteps as we begin our own path to happiness.

❋

For yesterday is already a dream, and tomorrow is only a vision, but today, well lived, makes every yesterday a dream of happiness, and every tomorrow a vision of hope.

❋

I want to love, cherish, and grow old with you.

The tides shall cease to beat the shore,
The stars fall from the sky;
Yet I will love thee more and more
Until the day I die, my dear,
Until the day I die.

ROBERT BURNS

*

I love thee, I love but thee with a love that shall not die,
Till the sun grows cold and the stars grow old.

WILLIAM SHAKESPEARE

*

Months and years may pass us by
But you are captured in my mind's eye
Looking and remaining the beauty you are today.

*

Tear up the calendar, for today time stood still.

*

Good knots have no rope but cannot be untied.

TAO TE CHING

A contract of eternal bond of love,
Confirm'd by mutual joining of hands,
Attested by the holy close of lips,
Strengthen'd by interchangement of rings
WILLIAM SHAKESPEARE

❋

I love you so much it hurts—may I never recover.

❋

I love thee with the breath, smile, tears, of all my life.
ELIZABETH BARRETT BROWNING

❋

Our union today doesn't signify the end of individuality,
only the beginning of a lifelong partnership.

❋

Whatever the future may bring, I promise I will treat
your love as my most treasured possession until the day
we must be parted.

In Bangladesh, after the wedding feast, the newlyweds are covered with a cloth. They feed each other food and share sips of a sacred drink under their covering. Then, as they look at their reflection in a mirror, they are each asked, "What do you see?", to which they should give a suitably romantic reply! Finally, they exchange garlands of flowers.

How long is forever?
Who wants to know?
Not I, not today.

❀

Marriage may be a contract, but it is more important
than any other enterprise. We two are the only
shareholders, both staking everything we have.

❀

I love you without knowing how or when or from where.
PABLO NERUDA

❀

The peace and serenity of the heavens be with us.
ADAPTED FROM A HAWAIIAN BLESSING

❀

Those who love deeply never grow old; they may die of
old age, but they die young.
AUTHOR UNKNOWN

As we touch each other's hearts, I promise to be gentle
and tender-hearted with you.

ADAPTED FROM TRADITIONAL ARYA SAMAJ RITUALS

❋

This day we shall remember for the rest of our lives; the
emotion will stay in our hearts forever.

❋

I marry you today in pursuit of a sacred love.

❋

Our simple ceremony will be over in minutes;
the sentiments will remain with us all our lives.

❋

Only our love hath no decay;
This no tomorrow hath, nor yesterday
Running it never runs from us away,
But truly keeps his first, last, everlasting day.

JOHN DONNE

Our lives before now are not over, they are just coming to a glorious crossroads.

***

May happiness be our companion and our days together be good and long upon the earth.

ADAPTED FROM AN APACHE BLESSING

***

We honor water to clean and soothe our relationship that it may never thirst for love.

CHEROKEE PRAYER

***

I want to spend every moment of every day with you for the rest of my life (then we ought to talk about putting things on a more permanent footing).

***

Even though you are mine, and I am yours, we can both still look at other people—if only to measure them against perfection.

I promise to work alongside you to build a better future.

❅

We find rest in those we love and we provide a resting place in ourselves for those who love us.
SAINT BERNARD OF CLAIRVAUX

❅

May we two find in each other the love for which all men and women long.

❅

A perfect woman nobly planned,
To warm, to comfort, and command;
And yet a spirit still and bright
With something of angelic light.
WILLIAM WORDSWORTH

❅

Never try to explain our love, let our joy and happiness speak for itself.

In a Japanese Shinto wedding ceremony, the ritual of drinking sake which dates back to the eighth century, is as important as any words spoken. Serving girls dressed in red and white dresses are in charge of stacking three cups in front of the bride and groom. The bride and groom each takes three sips from each cup, three times. It is at this moment that they are considered to be married. Sake is then served to the members of both families to celebrate the union.

I promise never to forsake you or these
solemn vows we make today.

＊

One word frees us of all the weight and
pain of life: that word is love.
SOPHOCLES

＊

Forever is a long time, but will it be long enough?

＊

A happy man marries the girl he loves,
A happier man loves the girl he marries.
ANONYMOUS

＊

Love is the river of life in the world.
HENRY WARD BEECHER

True love is more than flirting, romance, and passion—
it is spending the rest of my life with you.

❊

Love is the beauty of the soul.
SAINT AUGUSTINE

❊

I am always conscious of my nearness to you,
your presence never leaves me. In you I have
a measure for every woman, for everyone;
in your love a measure for all that is to be.
JOHANN WOLFGANG VON GOETHE

❊

Love means nothing in tennis but it is everything in life.
AUTHOR UNKNOWN

❊

This journey shall turn to our greater love.
HOMER

Let curiosity be replaced by reassurance, until we blend
together without noticing the joins.

✳

I more than love you and cannot cease to love you.
LORD BYRON

✳

Now that we know the strength of shared faith and
feelings—let the future begin.

✳

Now that we know the power of a true and loving
relationship—let it never end.

✳

None shall part us from each other
One in life and death are we
All in all to one another
I to thee and thou to me.
WILLIAM S. GILBERT

A man is often too young to marry,
but he is never too old to love.

FINNISH PROVERB

✳

Some love lasts a lifetime; true love lasts forever.

AUTHOR UNKNOWN

✳

Marriage is about faith, hope, and love,
but the greatest of these is love.

✳

Men always want to be a woman's first love. That is their
clumsy vanity. We women have a more subtle instinct
about things. What we like is to be a man's last romance.

OSCAR WILDE

✳

I vow with all the life coursing through my body
and all the love in my heart to be yours and yours
only until the end of our days.

In Italy, the groom's tie is traditionally cut into pieces by the best man and each piece is sold or auctioned off at the wedding to help pay for the honeymoon. Alternatively, the bride might carry a satin bag in which guests place envelopes of money to help fund a lavish ceremony. Either the bride's grandmother guards this bag during the festivities or the bride wears it so that male guests can put money in it in exchange for a dance with her.

Ah my beloved, fill the cup that clears
Today of past regrets and future fears.
OMAR KHAYYAM

*

Your love for me is as vital to me as the food
I eat—but even more sustaining.

*

I pledge to you my living and dying, equally in your care.
ANCIENT CELTIC VOW

*

There is no remedy for love but to love more.
HENRY DAVID THOREAU

*

No sooner met but they looked;
No sooner looked but they loved;
No sooner loved but they sighed;
No sooner sighed but they asked one another the reason;
No sooner knew the reason but they sought the remedy.
WILLIAM SHAKESPEARE

There is only one happiness in life: to love and be loved.
GEORGE SAND

✳

Real love stories never have an ending.
ANONYMOUS

✳

Love is a symbol of eternity that wipes away
all sense of time, removing all memory of a
beginning and all fear of an end.
IKHIDE OSHOMA

✳

For you see each day I love you more
Today more than yesterday and less than tomorrow.
ROSEMONDE GERARD

✳

I used to live to work, now I work so that I have
somewhere to come home to you from.

In the Philippines, a witness may pin the bride's veil to the groom's shoulder to symbolize unity. A white cord may also be hung around the couple's necks emphasizing the eternal bond between them. The newlyweds then light two candles on either side of a unity candle. Lastly, the groom gives his bride 13 coins that have been blessed by the priest, a rite which is believed to promote loyalty and prosperity.

From this day forth, you will make my life
as beautiful as my dreams.

＊

A heart as soft, a heart as kind
A heart as sound and free
As in the whole world thou canst find
That heart I'll give to thee.
ROBERT HERRICK

＊

Love is something eternal. The aspect may
change but not the essence.
VINCENT VAN GOGH

＊

I promise to be the same woman (man) you marry
today—tomorrow and forever.

＊

Love is an ideal thing, marriage a real thing.
JOHANN WOLFGANG VON GOETHE

Not an angel dwells above
Half so fair as her O love.
JOHN VANBRUGH

✳

My love for you is as high as the sky, as deep as the sea, as
tall as a mountain, as pure as an innocent child's.

✳

My thoughts of you are like flowing water,
will they ever have an end?
HSU KAN

✳

As I looked into your eyes, a bright, wonderful
future winked right back.

✳

Flesh of flesh,
Bone of my bone thou art, and from thy state
Mine never shall be parted, bliss or woe.
JOHN MILTON

I love you unconditionally—on condition
that you love me back forever.

✳

Tho' I were doom'd to wander on
Beyond the sea, beyond the sun,
Till my last, weary sand was run—
Till then—and then I love thee.

ROBERT BURNS

✳

My heart is high above, my body full of bliss
For I am set in luve as well as I would wiss
I luve my lady pure and she luvis me again
I am her serviture, she is my soverane.

ANONYMOUS

✳

You touch all my senses, but most of all
you touch my soul.

I saw Eternity the other night
Like a great ring or pure and endless light
All calm, as it was bright.
HENRY VAUGHAN

*

May love keep us joined at the hip, and may
respect keep us independent of mind.

*

Give a man a girl he can love,
As I, O my love, love thee,
And his heart is great with the pulse of fate
At home, on land, on sea.
JAMES THOMSON

*

I can promise you a future of happiness without
fear of failure, because mine is now assured and I am
solely responsible for yours.

Love conquers all things; let us too surrender to love.

VIRGIL

✳

If love and honor plus trust and commitment is the equation for true happiness, add two and multiply this by every day for the rest of our lives.

✳

There was never any yet that wholly could escape love, and never shall there be any, never so long as beauty shall be, never so long as eyes can see.

LONGUS

✳

Doubt thou the stars are fire;
Doubt that the sun doth move;
Doubt truth to be a liar;
But never doubt I love.

WILLIAM SHAKESPEARE

Never change when love has found its home.
PROPERTIUS

❄

Harmony is pure love, for love is complete agreement.
LOPE DE VEGA

❄

Every day is a new beginning.
May you live all the days of your lives.
JONATHAN SWIFT

❄

The pleasure of love is in loving. We are happier in the
passion we feel than in that we arouse.
FRANÇOIS, DUC DE LA ROCHEFOUCAULD

❄

You are the only person in the world I cannot
face the future without.

Some marriages in northern Egypt take place at night. The wedding guests walk in a lively procession to the church, the men carrying lanterns and the women singing. Once at the church, the priest ties a silk cord around the groom, and recites prayers, before untying the groom again. He uses the cord to tie the two wedding rings together, then he undoes the knot, before placing the rings on the couple's fingers.

Three little words that carry such weight: I love you.

＊

Love is my religion and I could die for that.
I could die for you.
JOHN KEATS

＊

He is not a lover, who does not love forever.
EURIPIDES

＊

I love you—those three words have my life in them.
ALEXANDREA, CZARINA TO NICHOLAS III

＊

If thou must love me, let it be for naught
Except for love's sake only
…that evermore thou mayst love on,
Through love's eternity.
ELIZABETH BARRETT BROWNING

The tragedy of love is not that it ends so soon, but that
we wait so long to begin it.
ANONYMOUS

✳

We look forward to the time when the power of
love will replace the love of power. Then will
our world know the blessing of peace.
WILLIAM GLADSTONE

✳

There is nothing like a dream to create a future.
VICTOR HUGO

✳

Twenty years from now you will be more
disappointed with the things you didn't do than
by the ones you did do.
MARK TWAIN

✳

Hold a true friend with both
your hands and never let go.
ADAPTED FROM A NIGERIAN PROVERB

In the Middle Ages, the Celts demonstrated their unity with handfasting. A year after this ritual was performed, the couple was considered husband and wife. In some African tribal cultures, a couple pledging marriage vows would have their hands bound together with braided grass to symbolize their union.

Love is an act of endless forgiveness, a tender
look which becomes a habit.
PETER USTINOV

✳

Our love may be like the ebb and incoming tide
of the ocean, but it will always flow.
FROM A SELECTION OF VOWS AT WWW.BWEDD.COM

✳

As the sun makes ice melt, kindness causes
misunderstanding, mistrust, and hostility to evaporate.
ALBERT SCHWEITZER

✳

Never apologize for showing feeling. When you do,
you apologize for the truth.
BENJAMIN DISRAELI

✳

When you are a child, forever is forever.
When you become an adult, forever is a relative term.
With you, I become a child again.

I promise to keep the good memories
alive and to let the bad ones die.

FROM A SELECTION OF VOWS AT WWW.BWEDD.COM

✳

Let those love now, who never loved before.
Let those who always loved, now love the more.

ANONYMOUS

✳

I promise to love you and only you, until the
day we are finally parted.

✳

An old man in love is like a flower in winter.

CHINESE PROVERB

✳

Marriage is like a golden ring in a chain,
whose beginning is a glance and whose ending is eternity.

KAHLIL GIBRAN

CHAPTER SIX
FOR RICHER,
FOR POORER

"NO ONE SAID IT WOULD BE EASY." THESE WORDS can easily be applied to marriage. Similarly, the wedding day itself may seem like a fairy tale but, there's a lot to be said for believing in a few harmless, age-old superstitions to bring a little light relief and good fortune when you finally walk down the aisle.

Good-luck charms and bad omens run through every culture and can bring some fun to the proceedings providing nervous brides don't get too worked up about their seriousness! The folk of the Appalachian mountains used to believe that it was bad luck to bathe on your wedding day. The Chinese also thought bathing on the day was not as auspicious as having a special bath the night before, infused with a type of grapefruit to guard against bad spirits. Most brides today would risk it, I think, rather than get married without a bath! Animals, too, have always carried their own significance to superstitious people and seeing a black cat, a dove, or a lamb was traditionally thought to bring a bride luck on her wedding day, yet a pig, a hare, or a lizard was a bad omen. A rainbow was a good sign, but the rain itself wasn't.

Like horoscopes, most of us only want to believe in superstitions when they are good ones. The same goes for wedding traditions. If we do see a chimney sweep on the day of our wedding, we're suddenly great fans of old sayings and beliefs—until we see a funeral procession or a freshly dug grave which are meant to bring bad luck, and then it's all stuff and nonsense.

Despite the "signs" however, the reality is that marriage has its peaks and its troughs—it's "richer and poorer." For a bride and groom to stand up publicly and acknowledge that there will be bad times as well as good in their vows may seem surprising, but it simply shows how deeply they have thought about their future together, and it underlines the commitment they are prepared to put into their lifelong plans. Even the most die-hard romantics among us appreciate that the course of true love doesn't run smoothly: working through adversity and the inevitable rough patches in a relationship is what seals a couple's bond and confirms their long-lasting compatibility.

There are lots of traditional and contemporary ideas to fit the theme of the rough and the smooth in this chapter. This is also a good place to bring in some light-heartedness. The point of these particular vows is not to dwell on the trials and tribulations of relationships, but to emphasize the strength of your love for each other. This is supposed to be a most joyous day and laughter is, after all, the best remedy for many things.

If you accept all things whether painful or joyful, you
will always know that you belong to each other.
TAO TE CHING

*

I promise to try to see things from your perspective—
even if I don't like the view.

*

I will always strive to make you feel happy and secure.
If I am guilty of anything, it will be of loving too much.

*

From now on we go the same way, in the same
direction, agreeing not to leave each other lonely,
or discouraged, or behind.
AUTHOR UNKNOWN

*

Here is my hand to hold with you, to bind us for life so
that I'll grow old with you.
TRADITIONAL IRISH VOW

In a traditional Lithuanian ceremony, couples often taste wine, salt, and then bread to symbolize the happiness, tears, and work that come with marriage. At a Yoruba wedding, the bride and groom taste four contrasting flavors which symbolize the different sentiments in a relationship: vinegar (bitter), lemon (sour), cayenne (hot), and honey (sweet). Like the Lithuanian tradition, the purpose of this ritual is to highlight that marriage brings both happiness and hardship.

I promise you my deepest love, my fullest devotion,
my most tender care.

*

Through all of the uncertainties and trials of the present
and future, I promise to be faithful and love you.

*

I promise to laugh with you, and cry with you, and grow
with you in mind and spirit.

*

You can ride out the storms when clouds hide the face of
the sun in your lives—remember that even if you lose
sight of it for a moment, the sun is still there.
APACHE BLESSING

*

We have our love to keep us warm.

I vow to love you without reservation and work together
with you to realize all our goals and dreams.

❋

Who, being loved, is poor?
OSCAR WILDE

❋

When life gets hard we must never forget there would be
no rainbows if there wasn't occasional rain.

❋

I will help you realize your strengths and learn from
them. I will help you recognize your weaknesses and
overcome them.

❋

Our love will never be overshadowed by the common,
nor obscured by the ordinary.

The tradition of the bridal veil may date back to Roman times, when it was thought that a veil would disguise the bride from evil spirits that might bring bad luck. Nowadays, it is thought that wearing the old veil of a happily married woman is lucky, and many brides choose to wear their mother's or grandmother's.

May the happiness we share today stay with us always.
May it illuminate our pleasures and shine
light on our pain.

*

Love is composed of a single soul inhabiting two bodies.
ARISTOTLE

*

You learn that love, true love
Always has joys and sorrow,
Seems ever present
Yet is never quite the same,
Becoming more than love and less than love,
So difficult to define.
And you learn that through it all
You really can endure,
That you really are strong
That you do have value.
ANONYMOUS

*

When the going gets tough, the tough stick together.

When the world seems against us, I promise to stand
with you hand in hand, shoulder to shoulder.

✳

In the end these things matter most;
How well did you love? How fully did you love?
How deeply did you learn to let go?
TRADITIONAL BUDDHIST TEACHING

✳

When we struggle to make sense of the world, pray that
we may never lose our sense of us.

✳

True love is a durable fire
In the mind ever burning
Never sick, never old, never dead
From itself never turning.
SIR WALTER RALEIGH

✳

Love teaches even asses to dance.
AUTHOR UNKNOWN

After the bride and groom have completed their wedding vows in Croatia, the bride's female relatives remove her veil and replace it with a scarf and apron while singing to her—these represent her new status as a wife. Then all the guests walk three times around a well which represents the holy trinity and throw apples into it to ensure the couple's fertility.

Our marriage will provide love and friendship, help and comfort, in times of joy and times of hardship.

*

Through illness or sorrow in coming years,
I will mop your brow and wipe your tears.

*

When two spiders unite they can tie up a lion.
ETHIOPIAN PROVERB

*

I take thee to be my husband (wife), loving what I know of you and trusting what I have yet to learn.

*

There is no greater invitation to love than loving first.
SAINT AUGUSTINE

*

Love can survive only by being born again and again.

I promise to share in your failures as well
as your fortunes.

*

May we always cherish each other as special and
unique individuals, respect each other's thoughts and
ideas, and be able to forgive.

*

[Love] adds a precious seeing to the eye
A lover's eyes will gaze an eagle blind.
A lover's ear will hear the lowest sound.
WILLIAM SHAKESPEARE

*

I promise to face each fear with a smile.

*

You and you no cross shall part
You and you are heart in heart.
WILLIAM SHAKESPEARE

In Sweden, a bride's mother gives her a gold coin to go in her right shoe, and her father provides a silver coin for her left. These tokens are believed to ensure that the couple will always be prosperous. This custom would be frowned upon in Italy where it was traditionally considered bad luck for a bride to have any gold on her during her wedding other than her wedding band.

If I'm prosperous, share in my fortune,
If I'm applauded, share in my fame.
If I end up a no one with nothing,
I'm still rich if you love me the same.

＊

Life will not always be perfect. To live an ideal life now
leaves us nothing to strive for.

＊

In the future, happy occasions will come as surely as the
morning. Difficult times will come as surely as the night.
TRADITIONAL BUDDHIST TEACHING

＊

Who needs a large measure of trust when
a little goes so far?

＊

Union gives strength.
AESOP

What greater thing is there for two human souls
than to feel that they are joined together to
strengthen each other in all labor.
GEORGE ELIOT

＊

Patience is a virtue, find it if you can
Sometimes in a woman, but less so in a man.

＊

Learn the wisdom of compromise, for it is better
to bend a little than to break.
JANE WELLS

＊

Love is an act of creation; a direct sharing of a process.

＊

We do not promise each other a rose garden that consists
entirely of beautiful flowers—we realize that there may
be one or two thorns.

What's mine is yours and what's yours is mine.
WILLIAM SHAKESPEARE

❋

May we always make an effort so that our
love never becomes one.

❋

May we find within us the courage to resist the many
pitfalls where love may stumble.

❋

Wherever there may be jealousy, let reason prevail.

❋

What earthly thing more can I crave?
What would I wish more at my will?
Nothing on earth more would I have
Save that I have to have it still.
SIR THOMAS WYATT

Together we will dream. We may be disappointed, but we will be disappointed together.

✳

The firmest faith is found in fewest words.

SIR EDWARD DYER

✳

If thou be foul, I shall make thee clean;
If thou be sick, I shall thee heal.

ANONYMOUS

✳

With you by my side, I can face good luck and bad with equal grace and acceptance.

✳

In wealth and woe, ever I support.

ANONYMOUS

In an ancient wedding custom, a loaf of wheat bread was broken over the bride's head to encourage a fertile and fulfilling life. The guests ate the crumbs which were believed to bring good luck. Similarly, after newlyweds in Iran have exchanged vows, crumbs from two decorated sugar cones are sometimes shaved over their heads for good luck.

For the Tiv, an Equatorial people of Africa, the wedding feast is a monumental affair. The meal of chicken cooked with sesame seeds combines universal symbols of fertility, but the most important aspect of the meal is the preparation. The birds must be caught by the groom himself, his mother, brothers or young men of his own age, while the sauce ingredients must be provided by his sisters, mother, and the wives of his father's friends. Then the meal is cooked by the homestead's married men.

If love be strong, hot, mighty and fervent
There may be no trouble, grief, or sorrow fall.
SIR THOMAS MORE

✳

Love is the plant of peace and most precious of virtues.
WILLIAM LANGLAND

✳

Love never mocks, truth never lies.
PHINEAS FLETCHER

✳

A strong marriage is built from many things—hope,
honor, fidelity, and trust—but must be built on the
strongest of all foundations, love.

✳

I would rather negotiate a rocky path with you than
tread a smooth path alone.

All that I have I bring
All that I am I give.
CHRISTINA ROSSETTI

✳

Never doubt my love.

✳

There is a comfort in the strength of love;
'Twill make a thing endurable, which else
Would break the heart.
WILLIAM WORDSWORTH

✳

Nothing in the world is single
All things by a law divine
In one another's being mingle—
Why not I with thine?
PERCY BYSSHE SHELLEY

✳

Love is hard work and hard work sometimes hurts
UNKNOWN

We have weathered storms and basked in the sunshine,
whatever the future, our forecast is bright.

✳

We honor wind and ask that we may sail through life
safe and calm as in our father's arms.

CHEROKEE PRAYER

✳

We resolve to accept each other's vices and virtues with
equal understanding.

✳

Love is like the dew that falls on both nettles and lilies.

SWEDISH PROVERB

✳

Without love, the rich and poor live in the same house.

AUTHOR UNKNOWN

A man is not where he lives but where he loves.
LATIN PROVERB

❋

True love is like ghosts, which everybody talks
about and few have seen.
FRANÇOIS, DUC DE LA ROCHEFOUCAULD

❋

No road is long with good company.
TURKISH PROVERB

❋

Look for a sweet person. Forget rich.
ESTÉE LAUDER

❋

True love is putting someone up on a pedestal, but still
being there to catch them when they fall.

In ancient Rome, the month of June was considered a lucky month to marry as it was named after Juno, the goddess of marriage, love, and happiness. Queen Victoria considered the month of May to be unlucky ("marry in May and rue the day") and also agreed that June was a fortuitous month. Traditionally, ministers would not perform a wedding during the months of Lent so February to April were forbidden.

At British weddings, tradition has it that if a bride passes a chimney sweep on her wedding day and kisses her on the cheek, she will have a happy and lucky marriage. Custom also dictates that if the best man is required to settle the fee with the minister on the wedding day, it is considered a good omen to pay an odd rather than an even amount.

Marry in September's shine,
Your living will be rich and fine.
If in October you do marry,
Love will come but riches tarry.
TRADITIONAL ENGLISH RHYME

✳

He that marries for wealth sells his liberty.
SIXTEENTH-CENTURY SAYING

✳

Today isn't perfect, because that would leave us little to
strive for, but it is a taste of how much better life can get.

✳

May all our problems be little ones.

✳

Better to be fortunate than rich.
IRISH PROVERB

Never love unless you can
Bear with all the faults of man.
THOMAS CAMPION

❊

Grant that we may never be irritated by the
quirks and idiosyncracies that we find so
appealing in each other today.

❊

I pray that we can be lucky in love if nothing else,
because no amount of money can match the
happiness I feel today.

❊

Love is not to be purchased, and affection has no price.
SAINT JEROME

❊

Where there's marriage without love, there will be love
without marriage.
BENJAMIN FRANKLIN

In Korea, the bride gives her groom's parents gifts of dates and chestnuts which are considered symbols of children. In exchange, the parents give her some sake, and then throw back at her the dates and chestnuts which she tries to catch in her wedding skirt.

In the Middle Ages, couples thought it unlucky if the bride's new surname began with the same letter as her maiden name, shown in the old rhyme: "Change the name and not the letter, marry for worse and not for better." In modern-day marriages, the trend is still for the wife to take her husband's surname, but in some rare cases, the husband has been known to take the wife's name.

Thrice happy they who through life's varied tide
With equal pace and gentle motion glide,
Whom, though the wave of fortune sinks or swells,
One reason governs and one wish impels.
THOMAS BLACKLOCK

※

Better is poverty in the hand of God
Than riches in the storehouse.
Better are loaves when the heart is joyous
Than riches in unhappiness.
EGYPTIAN SAYING

※

Our hoard is little but our hearts are great.
ALFRED, LORD TENNYSON

※

We may be poor of purse, but we will
always be rich of heart.

Marriage is a contract I will happily sign. When our way becomes difficult I promise to stand by you and uplift you, so that through our union we can accomplish more than we could alone.

FROM A SELECTION OF VOWS AT WWW.BWEDD.COM

❋

Love and forgiveness go hand-in-hand, one would not be possible without the other.

❋

If you love the good you see in another, you make it your own.

SAINT GREGORY THE GREAT

❋

I shall not set the snares today for your love has caught me.

ANCIENT EGYPTIAN SAYING

❋

About those worldly goods you'd like to share: no man needs to hoard that much vinyl!

A marriage should always reflect the effort put into it,
without it actually becoming an effort.

*

Marriages are made in heaven. Then again, so are
thunder, lightning, tornadoes, and hail!
AUTHOR UNKNOWN

*

The pessimist sees difficulty in every opportunity.
The optimist sees the opportunities in every difficulty.

*

The supreme happiness of life is the conviction
of being loved for yourself or, more correctly,
being loved in spite of yourself.
ANONYMOUS

*

When you are in the mood,
I will always be close.
If you are in a mood,
I'll come back later…

CHAPTER SEVEN
PARTNERS
on
ALL LEVELS

IN THE OPENING CHAPTER OF HIS CLASSIC NOVEL, *The Mayor of Casterbridge*, Thomas Hardy's eponymous hero sells his wife for the price of a drink. Granted, this is obviously a work of fiction, but it does underline the way marriage was often viewed in the past. For many centuries, and in many cultures, daughters and sometimes sons were seen as chattels to be disposed of wherever their families saw fit. Dowries were set between families, tribes, or clans so that the groom's family gained not only a daughter-in-law, but also land, possessions, power, or money as "compensation" for taking her into their fold. Royal children particularly were moved from state to state, like pawns in a chess game, for political advantage.

Little girls may have dreamed of the fairytale prince who would come along on his horse and whisk them away to happy-ever-after, but marriages were often viewed as business deals rather than love matches. They still are in some parts of the world, of course, and many brides and grooms are quite happy to respect their cultural heritage and follow the tradition of an arranged match. Not all arranged marriages are without love, however, and not all love matches turn out to be perfect either. Some individuals will still marry for money, security, or some particular reason other than being passionately in love with their partner because that's the way of the world, but for the couple marrying for no better reason than the fact that they cannot visualize a future without the one they love, marriage is an equal partnership and there are many ways to express this in your ceremony.

The decision to marry is based on many things—from romance and passion, to understanding, companionship, and shared interests. You are not just lovers, but best friends too. You are a couple, but you are also individuals who deserve respect and sometimes need their own space. There's an old British joke that when a bride runs through the order of her wedding ceremony at the rehearsal, she can often be heard muttering "aisle … altar … hymn, aisle … altar … hymn," until it becomes, "I'll … alter … him, I'll … alter … him" yet getting married isn't supposed to be about changing the person you love. It's about growing and developing together and, hopefully, the following suggested vows emphasize this. Everybody has to work at some level to keep a marriage fresh—unfortunately, it's not all hearts and flowers, even for the most love-struck. So start as you mean to go on, by reading each other a specially chosen piece of love poetry— it's just about the most wonderful thing two best friends can do on their wedding day!

Today my best friend becomes my husband (wife).

＊

May our hands be forever clasped in friendship and our hearts forever joined in love.

＊

May every day that we continue to grow together— as partners and allies, confidantes and friends— end with a kiss.

＊

Wanted: one roommate on a permanent basis. Good sense of humor essential.

＊

Friendship is the marriage of the soul.
VOLTAIRE

The tradition of wearing a buttonhole to complement the bride's flowers stems from the chivalric days when a knight wore his lover's colors as a sign of devotion. In Scotland today, it is traditional for the groom and his wedding party to wear boutonnières of white heather which denotes good luck and a long-lasting union that, like this hardy Scottish flower, can weather any storm.

Two parts of a loving whole.
Two hearts and a single soul.

AUTHOR UNKNOWN

＊

A husband is someone who will share his hopes
and aspirations, his bed, his pension,
and his last piece of chewing gum
with the woman he loves.

＊

My bounty is as boundless as the sea,
My love as deep; the more I give to thee.

WILLIAM SHAKESPEARE

＊

From this day forward I promise to share with
you the secrets of my heart.

Close your heart to every love but mine;
hold no one in your arms but me.

SONG OF SONGS 8: 66-67, THE BIBLE

*

I look forward to being your friend, companion,
and lover for life.

*

The more love we receive, the more love we shine forth.

DANTE

*

What greater thing is there on this earth than for two
souls to be joined as one?

*

I was always searching for someone like you to make my
life complete—I just didn't know it.

Immediately after a traditional Jewish ceremony, the couple is often left alone for a few moments to reflect on the vows they have made and the promise of the future. Originally, it was symbolic of a time when the couple could consummate the marriage and is known as Yichud. *The couple has been fasting since the morning, but now they can break their fast and the feasting can begin.*

Love is all we have, the only way that each
can help the other.
EURIPIDES

＊

Journeys end in lovers meeting.
WILLIAM SHAKESPEARE

＊

I promise to share with you my hopes, my fears,
and the secrets of my soul.

＊

This day I marry my best friend...the one I live for
because the world seems brighter, as our happy times are
better and our burdens feel much lighter.
AUTHOR UNKNOWN

＊

Thank you for being what you are to me.
I cherish our friendship and will love you today,
tomorrow, and forever.

Love demands everything and rightly so.

LUDWIG VAN BEETHOVEN

※

I promise always to respect the special bond
that ties us together.

※

It is the man and woman united that makes
the complete human being.

BENJAMIN FRANKLIN

※

As you have pledged to me your life and love,
so I happily give you mine.

※

To live with the woman a man loves is of all
lives the most complete and free.

ROBERT LOUIS STEVENSON

May we teach each other what we are now
and what we can become.

*

You don't marry someone you live with—you marry
the person you cannot live without.
ANONYMOUS

*

Life has taught us that love doesn't consist in
gazing at each other but in looking outward
together in the same direction.
ANTOINE DE SAINT-EXUPÉRY

*

In letting me love you and loving me in return, you have
shown me the deep joy of putting someone else first.

*

Today is the first day of our new life together.

If friendship is firmly established between two hearts,
they do not need to exchange vows.

✳

Love is a fruit in season at all times and
within reach of every hand.

MOTHER TERESA

✳

If I could write the beauty of your eyes,
And in fresh numbers number all your graces,
The age to come would say "This poet lies."

WILLIAM SHAKESPEARE

✳

Hand in hand as we stood
'Neath the shadows of the wood
Heart to heart as we lay
In the dawning of the day.

ROBERT BRIDGES

✳

Hold my hand but cherish my heart.

To demonstrate togetherness, the bride and groom at a Thai wedding will sit close together on the floor. Their hands are linked by a chain of flowers. A senior guest will soak the couple's hands in water from a conch shell and wish them good luck.

For this is the golden morning of love,
And you are his morning star.
ALFRED, LORD TENNYSON

✳

Love is the perfect sum of all delight.
ANONYMOUS

✳

When the one man loves the one woman, and the woman
loves the one man, the very angels desert heaven and sit
in that house and sing for joy.
THE KAMA SUTRA

✳

Our hearts and spirits are entwined as one.

✳

You will be my one and only lover, always.
This is my solemn vow.
ANONYMOUS

As our love grew stronger, I entrusted you with my hopes and dreams. Today the hopes have been realized and the dreams have come true.

※

Drinke to me onely, with thine eyes,
And I will pledge with mine;
Or leave a kisse but in the cup
And I'll not look for wine.
BEN JONSON

※

I promise to praise your achievements, laugh at your jokes, and keep you warm on cold nights.

※

Thy love is such I can no way repay
The heavens reward thee manifold I pray.
ANNE BRADSTREET

※

You are my past, my present, and my future.

*As part of the Mexican wedding ceremony,
a lasso or a length of rosary beads (or even a
garland of orange blossoms) is wound
around the necks of the bride and groom in
a figure of eight. In an alternative gesture,
one set of parents may bless a double rosary
or lasso and give it to the couple. The lasso
is worn for the remainder of the service,
then taken off and given to the bride in
commemoration of her becoming the
mistress of her groom's heart and home.*

Remember that true friendship is the basis for any lasting relationship. The person you choose to marry is deserving of the courtesies and kindnesses you bestow on your friends.

JANE WELLS

﹡

Between a man and his wife nothing ought to rule but love. As love ought to bring them together, so it is the best way to keep them well together.

WILLIAM PENN

﹡

We come together to celebrate a discovery and to record in the minds and hearts of all present the ripe event of a love that has bloomed.

METHODIST CEREMONY

﹡

Today I give my life to the most wonderful person I have ever met.

Light, so low in the vale
You flash and lighten afar,
For this is the golden morning of love
And you are his morning star.
ALFRED, LORD TENNYSON

✳

I wonder by my troth, what thou and I
Did, till we loved? Were we not weaned till then?
JOHN DONNE

✳

I never saw so sweet a face
As that I stood before
My heart has left its dwelling place
And can return no more.
JOHN CLARE

✳

I love you because you have influenced the way I feel
without ever trying to influence the way I think.

My life would have no rhyme or reason
without your love.

*

Grow to my lip, thou sacred kiss,
On which my soul's beloved swore
That there should come a time of bliss
When she would mock my hopes no more.
SIR THOMAS MORE

*

Marriage is a commitment between lovers, but also an
agreement between friends.

*

The greatest bliss
Is in a kiss—
A kiss of love refin'd
When springs the soul,
Without control,
And blends the bliss with mind.
CHARLOTTE DACRE

I want you to always know how much I treasure
the gift of your love.

❋

Love is patient, love is kind. It does not envy, it does not
boast, it is not proud. It is not rude, it is not self-seeking,
it is not easily angered, it keeps no record of wrongs.
CORINTHIANS 13:4–5, THE BIBLE

❋

Receive this love as a pledge of wedded
love and faithfulness.

❋

I have such faith in our marriage, I know that in ten,
twenty, or thirty years' time, I will feel the same flutter of
love and excitement when you enter a room as I did
when you entered this church today.

One Jewish tradition is for the bride to circle the groom seven times before joining him under the chupah. *This signifies both the seven days of creation and the seven wedding blessings. It also indicates that he is now the center of her world and she is the center of his. Couples nowadays often choose to circle each other to demonstrate their equality in the relationship.*

I am the sky, you are the earth
I am a song, you are the tune.
MAHARASHTRIAN RITUAL

❋

You touched my hand and I knew you were for me.

❋

We are two persons, but there is only one life before us.
May beauty surround us both on the journey ahead.
ADAPTED FROM AN APACHE BLESSING

❋

To you, my best friend, I give the ultimate token of
friendship, my life and soul.

❋

The most important thing in life is to love and be loved.

We honor fire and ask that our union be warm and
glowing with love in our hearts.

CHEROKEE PRAYER

※

A strong marriage depends on a genuine liking, an
unequaled passion, and an unswerving respect.

※

I planted a hand
And there came up a palm.
I planted a heart
And there came up a balm.

CHRISTINA ROSSETTI

※

Whatever our souls are made of, his
and mine are the same.

EMILY BRONTË

At a Tamil wedding, the groom's parents offer the bride a nine-yard sari. When the bride's sister-in-law and aunts have helped her to change into it, she sits on her father's lap. A farmer's yoke is then taken and touched against her forehead to reflect her and her husband's new journey, side by side, pulling the plough of life.

Thy love is better than high birth to me,
Richer than wealth, prouder than garments' cost
Of more delight than hawks or horses be;
And having thee, of all men's pride I boast.

WILLIAM SHAKESPEARE

❄

Those who wish to sing always find a song.
At the touch of a lover, everyone becomes a poet.

PLATO

❄

Fortune is like a woman—if you miss her today
think not to find her tomorrow.

NAPOLEON

❄

A friend is someone who knows all about you
and loves you just the same.

PROVERB

To be loved—be lovable.

OVID

✳

So much of what we learn of love we learn at home.

AUTHOR UNKNOWN

✳

Love built on beauty, soon as beauty, dies.

JOHN DONNE

✳

Side-by-side, hand-in-hand, hearts entwined. May we
grow closer every day so eventually no one, not even us,
will see the joins.

✳

You mold my hopes, you fashion me within.

SAMUEL TAYLOR COLERIDGE

Your hand in my hand
My soul inspired
My heart in bliss
Because we go together.
ANCIENT EGYPTIAN LOVE POEM

*

Love is like playing the piano. First you must
learn to play by the rules, then you must forget
the rules and play from the heart.
AUTHOR UNKNOWN

*

Love is thinking about each other more than
we think about ourselves.

*

If I could reach up and hold a star for every time
you've made me smile, the entire evening sky
would be in the palm of my hand.
AUTHOR UNKNOWN

Although I conquer all the earth,
yet for me there is only one city.
In that city is for me only one house,
And in that house, one room only,
And in that room a bed,
And one woman sleeps there,
The shining joy and jewel of my kingdom.
ANCIENT SANSKRIT WRITING

᛭

The only time you truly know yourself is when you allow
a friend and lover close enough to know you, too.

᛭

And I can think of nothing in life
That I could more wisely do
Than know a friend, and be a friend
And love a friend like you.
AUTHOR UNKNOWN

᛭

What a grand thing to be loved
What a grander thing still to love.
VICTOR HUGO

As a sign of their union, one Navajo Indian custom involved the couple sharing a meal of corn—white corn to represent the groom and yellow to signify the bride. The Greeks also share sacred food in a wedding ritual. The bride and groom take honey and walnuts from silver spoons. Walnuts break into four parts which represent the union of the bride and groom and their two families.

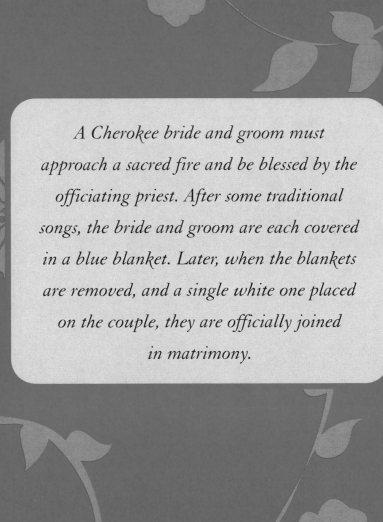

A Cherokee bride and groom must approach a sacred fire and be blessed by the officiating priest. After some traditional songs, the bride and groom are each covered in a blue blanket. Later, when the blankets are removed, and a single white one placed on the couple, they are officially joined in matrimony.

Came but for friendship and took away love.

THOMAS MOORE

✳

Love is like the sun coming out of the clouds and
warming your soul.

✳

I love you not only for what you are but for
what I am with you.

ELIZABETH BARRETT BROWNING

✳

All the love that history knows
Is said to be in every rose
Yet all that could be found in two
Is less than what I feel for you.

AUTHOR UNKNOWN

The fact that we found each other is a miracle, though I can't promise you any more. What I can promise you is loyalty, friendship, support, and love from this day and forever.

❋

The pearly treasures of the sea,
The lights that spatter heaven above,
More precious than these wonders are
My heart-of-hearts filled with your love.

HEINRICH HEINE

❋

Let us not look for trouble but hide from it. Let us promise never to take offense where none is intended, nor feel slighted without cause.

❋

But I send you a cream-white rosebud,
With a flash on its petal tips;
For the love that is purest and sweetest,
Has a kiss of desire on the lips.

JOHN BOYLE O'REILLY

Marry your like.
OVID

※

I love you. No three words can ever put it more
simply or more powerfully.

※

Thou art my life, my love, my heart
The very eyes of me:
And hast command of ever part
To love and die for thee.
ROBERT HERRICK

※

As equal partners, I will always strive to gain your
respect without seeking your approval.

※

Love is blind, but you've opened my eyes to the
beauty of the world.

Ask me no more where those stars light,
Than downwards fall in dead of night:
For in your eyes they sit, and there
Fixed become, as in their sphere.
THOMAS CAREW

※

As a child, your best friend is the most important
person in the world. As an adult, your best friend
is the person you marry.

※

We plaited our hair and became man and wife,
The love of us two was never in doubt
Let us enjoy the bliss of tonight,
Making merry while the good time lasts.
CHINESE WRITING, SECOND CENTURY

※

If at first you don't succeed, try a little ardour!
POPULAR GRAFFITI

A Colonial American bride would often stitch a small bag to her dress containing fabric, wood, corn, and a coin to represent future warmth, shelter, food, and prosperity. By the same token, a Scottish groom might keep some coins in his traditional sporran (small pouch at the front of the kilt) and after the ceremony, he can throw the loose change onto the ground for children to pick up. This amusing custom is called a scrammy!

The thali *in a Tamil wedding is a sacred pendant hung from a yellow thread, and is the equivalent of a wedding ring, to be worn for a lifetime. The* thali *consists of two pieces, one from each family. In some Tamil weddings the elders bless the* thali *and the groom ties two knots of the thread around the bride's neck. A third knot is done by the groom's sister.*

O God give the joy and God the love,
To those who are lovers true,
Shed down benediction from above
As in one are joined the two.
OLD GAELIC PRAYER

❋

Love, who is the most beautiful among the immortal
gods, the melter of limbs, overwhelms in their hearts the
intelligence and good counsel of all gods and all men.
HESIOD

❋

Love knows nothing of order.
SAINT JEROME

❋

A good heart is better than all the heads in the world.
EDWARD BULWER-LYTTON

True happiness consists not in the multitude of friends
But in the worth and choice.

BEN JONSON

＊

Love's mysteries in souls do grow
But yet the body is his book.

JOHN DONNE

＊

What is a kiss? Why this, as some approve
The sure, sweet cement, glue and lime of love.

ROBERT HERRICK

＊

Love is like a dizziness,
It winna let a poor body
Gang about his bizziness.

JAMES HOGG

＊

Let us always divide a task and share a joy.

Give me a kiss, and to that kiss a score.
Then to that twenty, add a hundred more:
A thousand to that hundred: so kiss on,
To make that thousand up a million.
Treble that million and when that is done,
Let's kiss afresh, as when we first begun.

ROBERT HERRICK

※

I promise to work at our love and always
make you a priority in my life.

FROM A SELECTION OF VOWS AT WWW.BWEDD.COM

※

I have chosen you to be my lover, my soulmate, my
friend, and I promise that I will never change my mind!

※

Lovers, like bees, live a honey-sweet life.

WRITTEN ON A WALL IN POMPEII

CHAPTER EIGHT
SUPPORT & COMMUNICATION

MUTUAL SUPPORT IS AN ESSENTIAL PART OF A HAPPY relationship. Promising to be supportive and protective of your lifelong partner is a big commitment—one of just many you will be making on your wedding day—but no less important than promising love and loyalty.

With our busy modern lives, there are always going to be times when one partner is busier or more distracted by work and may overlook the fact that the other person has a life outside the relationship too. Marriage is all about living two lives together and that includes finding time to listen to the other person.

Many wedding traditions emphasize the new bond formed between a man and a woman with symbolic gestures during the ceremony, from the binding of hands with embroidered cloth (popular in Eastern European cultures) to the ancient Filipino custom of pricking both partners with a thorn to draw blood before the couple holds hands. In many ceremonies the couple is joined together by anything from threads of cotton or a cloak, to a long chain of rosary beads or even a lasso, such as in Mexico. Whatever the method, the point being made universally is togetherness, and it underpins everything of importance in a wedding ceremony.

In the age of e-mails and multimedia, it is easy to underestimate the power of communicating one to one, and face to face, but it's a power that supersedes any other. By choosing to make a public pledge that you will always keep the channels of communication open between you, you are both promising not to take each other for granted. There are many ways to do this—from repeating heartfelt pledges never to go to bed on a disagreement, to more light-hearted vows that include not arguing over the television remote control or who switches off the light at night.

As well as making a promise to support your lifelong partner during the ceremony, it is always a nice touch to involve the friends and family you have invited to share your big day. In the Anglican wedding ceremony today, some ministers ask the congregation, "will you support (bride) and (groom) in their life together?" All your special guests then have to do is answer, "we will." Even just a few words of support from your loved ones make the whole day feel so much more inclusive. This final section of proposed vows looks at the art of communication with suggestions for lines to utter in church, but which can also be repeated in private, months and even years later, so that you and your partner always know what you mean to each other.

I love you so much; you are my right hand.

*

From this day forward,
You shall not walk alone,
My heart will be your shelter,
And my arms will be your home.
AUTHOR UNKNOWN

*

In the words of the song, I'll be there—
"always and forever."

*

May this be the start of a lifetime of trust and of
caring that's just now begun.

*

Here all seeking is over, the lost has been found.
A mate has been found to share the chills of winter.
ANCIENT HAWAIIAN WEDDING PRAYER

I take your hand today as my wife.
To loyally love and cherish for all of my life.

*

Never let the sun go down on your anger
They that are rich in words, in words discover
That they are poor in that which makes a lover.

SIR WALTER RALEIGH

*

As two we might have had twice the force.
As one we have at least twice the power.

*

I promise to share with you my hopes and fears
Why blush ye, love, to give to me your hand?

EDMUND SPENSER

*

I lie down with thee, I rise up with thee.

AZTEC LOVE SONG

I vow today that I will always listen rather than hear, and talk to you, instead of at you.

*

I promise never to go to sleep on an argument, so we will always start each new day together in harmony.

*

In marriage you do not lose yourself, you add something new.
WICCAN MARRIAGE CEREMONY

*

A problem shared is a problem halved.

*

Let's have a dance 'ere we are married, that we may lighten our own hearts and our wives' heels.
WILLIAM SHAKESPEARE

During a Malyali ceremony in Southern India, the couple sits around the sacred nuptial fire. The groom sits in front of the bride and tilts his head backwards to touch her forehead, symbolizing a meeting of minds. Then the bride offers a special kind of puffed rice into the fire, while reciting several mantras.

*

The main part of a Russian wedding is the reception which is often a grand two-day celebration with music, dancing, feasting, and drinking. One of the lively traditions which takes place during the reception sees the couple traditionally racing each other to a special carpet where they recite their vows; the first one there will supposedly have supremacy in the marriage.

I have chosen you, and you alone, to share my life.
It is not a choice undertaken lightly, but it is a
commitment deeply felt.

*

I vow, with my captive heart and rejoicing soul,
to love you for all my life.

*

Those bound by love must obey each other if they are to
keep company long. Love will not be constrained by
mastery. When mastery comes, the god of love at once
beats its wings and farewell, he is gone.
GEOFFREY CHAUCER

*

With deepest joy I receive you into my life that
together we may be one.

*

I promise to stand by you always and stay
close to you forever.

May the channels of communication always
work both ways.

✻

I give you all that I have myself, and my love.

✻

You have trusted me with your heart, I trust you
with my life. Let us always place trust at the
center of our relationship.

✻

If the eyes are perpetually restless, they cannot
appreciate a beautiful object set before them.
SAINT BASIL THE GREAT

✻

You are in my every waking thought and my
sweetest dreams. I wake up with a smile every day
simply because you are in my life.

True Love is inexhaustible; the more you give,
the more you have.

ANTOINE DE SAINT-EXUPÉRY

❋

We are gathered here to celebrate one of life's
greatest moments—to give recognition to the value
and beauty of love.

❋

Honor, riches, marriage-blessing,
Long continuance and increasing,
Hourly joys be still upon you!
Juno sings her blessings on you.

WILLIAM SHAKESPEARE

❋

I do love thee as each flower,
Loves the sun's life-giving power.

HENRY CONSTABLE DAMELUS

Love is like the wild rose-briar
Friendship like the holly tree—
The holly is dark when the rose-briar blooms
But which will bloom most constantly?
EMILY BRONTË

*

I promise to honor your culture and respect your
faith as you will honor and respect mine.

*

Each be other's comfort kind:
Deep, deeper than divined,
Divine charity, dear charity,
Fast you ever, fast bind.
GERARD MANLEY HOPKINS

*

Trust works both ways.
If you cannot trust, you cannot be trusted.

Red is the dominating color at a Chinese wedding. It signifies love, joy, prosperity, and is used on the invitations, to decorate both families' homes on the day, and often also to dress the bride. Tea also plays a central part in this special day: it is sometimes served to the elders to symbolically ask permission for the wedding to take place. At the end of their simple ceremony, Chinese couples traditionally bow to each other as a sign of respect.

I'm not marrying you because you are perfect, I am marrying you to discover all your little imperfections.

* * *

My face in thine eye, thine in mine appears.
JOHN DONNE

* * *

I won't always agree with what you think or say, but I will always respect your right to independent thought.

* * *

If ever two were one, then surely we
If ever man were lov'd by wife than thee
If ever wife was happy in a man
Compare with me ye woman if you can.
ANNE BRADSTREET

* * *

I promise to treat you with the respect
your behavior deserves!

Love looks not with the eyes, but with the mind.

WILLIAM SHAKESPEARE

※

May we always need each other, not to fill a void but to acknowledge our complete union.

※

Love is the joy of the good, the wonder of the wise, the amazement of the gods.

PLATO

※

Don't walk in front of me, I may not follow.
Don't walk behind me, I may not lead.
Walk beside me and just be my friend.

OLD IRISH PROVERB

※

By exchanging these vows, we can face new responsibilities together with confidence.

Let us agree never to let a day pass without a smile,
a word, a caress, and a kiss.

✻

Yes, love indeed is light from heaven;
A spark of that immortal fire
With angels shar'd, by Allah given
To lift from Earth our low desire.
LORD BYRON

✻

Words cannot express the pride I feel at becoming
your lifelong partner.

✻

Promise me that when you listen you will also hear.

✻

If marriage is a partnership, let us take care that one
partner is not always sleeping.

Love knows no jealousy and gives itself no
false airs or false pride.

*

[Love] always protects, always trusts, always
hopes, always perseveres.
I CORINTHIANS 13:7, THE BIBLE

*

The one who gives love is also the one who receives love.
ADAPTED FROM MAHARASHTRIAN RITUALS

*

This bond I have with you focuses all my dreams
and fulfills all my desires.

*

This is my earnest vow, based on hope, trust,
and understanding.

Treat yourselves and others with respect, and remind yourselves often of what brought you together.
APACHE BLESSING

❄

Take my hand—to work alongside you, to caress and soothe you, to hold firm.

❄

A car manufacturer's formula for a successful marriage: stick to one model!

❄

Combined, we will be better than we could ever be alone.

❄

Neither a lofty degree of intelligence nor imagination nor both together go into the making of genius. Love, love, love—that is the soul of genius.
WOLFGANG AMADEUS MOZART

So are you to my thoughts as food to life,
Or as sweet seasoned showers are to the ground.
WILLIAM SHAKESPEARE

❋

Love is not blind—it enables us to see things
that others fail to see.

❋

We are now taking into our care the happiness of the
one person we love best in the world.

❋

I promise never to try to change you. I cannot risk
losing all the wonderful things about you that I fell in
love with in the first place.

❋

You have helped me to see the world anew. You have
refreshed my outlook, diminished my cynicism, and
restored my faith in human nature.

Traditional German weddings can last three days. The first day is for the civil ceremony, the second is for the wedding party, and the last is devoted to the religious ceremony. In one custom, which takes place on the third day, the groom kneels on the hem of the bride's gown to show her who's boss, only for the bride to step on his foot as she gets up to show him she won't stand for it!

In the thirteenth century, a nobleman often gave his bride a love token such as a jewel. The woman, on the other hand, might well have offered her courtly lover a leash (presumably for one of his dogs, rather than as a precursor of their future together!). Modern-day love tokens usually include jewelry, mainly rings, but some couples choose to give each other a mere symbol of their love, such as a red rose.

If I have the gift of prophecy and can fathom all mysteries and all knowledge, and if I have faith that can move mountains, but have not love, I am nothing.

I CORINTHIANS 13:2, THE BIBLE

※

May we always strive to meet the commitment of marriage with the strength and spirit we feel as we make these vows today.

※

Love is space and time measured by the heart.

MARCEL PROUST

※

Marriage is one of the most important obligations that any two people can make in their lifetime.

※

I promise to share the burden of your worries without being the cause of too many.

When we need to, we will take on the world together.
May we each be like the air that inhabits the other.
APACHE BENEDICTION

❋

When you come home with good news,
I will welcome it.
When you come home with bad news,
I will share it.
When you come home with no news,
will you listen to mine?

❋

A smile is the light in the window of your face that
shows that your heart is at home.

❋

Absence diminishes small loves and increases
great ones, as the wind blows out the candle
and blows up the bonfire.
FRANÇOIS, DUC DE LA ROCHEFOUCAULD

Every heart sings a song, incomplete,
until another heart whispers back.
PLATO

✳

Shared joy is a double joy. Shared sorrow is half a sorrow.
SWEDISH PROVERB

✳

The sum which two married people owe
to one another defies calculation.
It is an infinite debt which can only be
discharged through all eternities.
JOHANN WOLFGANG VON GOETHE

✳

For nothing is greater or better than when man
and wife dwell in a home in one accord, a great gift
to their foes and joy to their friends.
HOMER

Love seeketh not itself to please
Nor for itself hath any care.
WILLIAM BLAKE

*

You cannot possess me, for I belong to myself.
But while we both wish it, I give you that which
is mine to give.
ANCIENT CELTIC SAYING

*

Since first I saw your face I resolved
To honor and renown you.
THOMAS FORD

*

To be selfish is easy, to be selfless is divine. May we both
keep our sense of self, yet put the other first.

*

May we always feel free to share our thoughts
and speak our minds.

In Egyptian society, shoes were often exchanged to seal the deal: the father of the bride gave the groom-to-be her shoes to confirm the marriage contract. In Anglo-Saxon times the groom would tap the heel of the bride's shoe to show his authority over her. Later in history, guests were known to throw shoes at newlyweds as they got into their carriage to bring good luck, which may be where the tradition of tying shoes to the back of the bridal car originated.

The real drawback to marriage is that
it makes one unselfish.
OSCAR WILDE

*

New things are made familiar and familiar
things made new.
SAMUEL JOHNSON

*

Two have more wit than one.
JOHN GOWER

*

It is easier to mend neglect than quicken love.
SAINT JEROME

*

There is no more lovely, friendly, and
charming relationship, communion, or
company than a good marriage.
MARTIN LUTHER

Love and a cough cannot be hid.
GEORGE HERBERT

❅

Lovers never get tired of each other, because they are
always talking about themselves.
FRANÇOIS, DUC DE LA ROCHEFOUCAULD

❅

Marriage has many pains, but celibacy has no pleasures.
SAMUEL JOHNSON

❅

Marriage resembles a pair of shears, so joined that they
cannot be separated; often moving in opposite directions,
yet always punishing anyone who comes between them.
SYDNEY SMITH

❅

The supreme happiness of life is the conviction
that we are loved.
VICTOR HUGO

In India, Sindhi couples are not allowed to see each other's faces during the ceremony. They sit facing each other and separated by a sheet, and place their feet on plates. The person who has the highest foot is believed to be the dominant one in the relationship.

*

To show a Highland groom was ready for the responsibility of marriage, an old Scottish custom saw the groom's friends fill a large basket (creel) full of stones. The groom would carry these on his back through the village until the bride came out to kiss him, ending the "creeling" ceremony.

Our chief want in life is somebody who
shall make us do what we can.
RALPH WALDO EMERSON

＊

It takes two to speak the truth—one to
speak and another to hear.
HENRY DAVID THOREAU

＊

Let us share pleasure and pain, the former
to ease the latter.

＊

To look up and not down,
To look forward and not back,
To look out and not in, and
To lend a hand.
EDWARD EVERETT HALE

＊

I love you for your sincerity, loyalty, integrity, and the
cute way your hair sticks up in the morning.

If either of us feels a wheel is about to come off,
let us make a promise to pull over and help
inspect the problem.

❋

'Tis a great confidence in a friend to tell him your faults;
greater still to tell him his.
BENJAMIN FRANKLIN

❋

Our relationship works so well because we always
bring out the best in each other, leaving no room for
weakness or doubt.

❋

Hope is the thing with feathers,
That perches in the soul,
And sings the tune without the words
And never stops—at all.
EMILY DICKINSON

When silence speaks for love she has much to say.
RICHARD GARNETT

✻

I ask that, throughout our lives together, you never tell
me what you think I want to hear, but tell me what you
are really thinking and feeling.

✻

The best way to love is to love like you
have never been hurt.
ANONYMOUS

✻

Love is like a butterfly, hold it too tight and it will be
crushed, hold it too loose and it will fly away.
AUTHOR UNKNOWN

✻

To the rest of the world, you might just be one person,
but to one special person, you might just be the world.

I promise to laugh with you during happy times,
not at you during bad.

※

Love is a canvas furnished by nature and
embroidered by imagination.
VOLTAIRE

※

Let us promise to greet each morning with a smile and
end each day with "I love you."

※

From this day forward, may we never sleep—
or wake—alone again.

※

Love has nothing to do with what you are
expecting to get, it's about what you are expected to
give—and that is everything.

As our lives together become more familiar, may they also retain mutual respect, so that we can feel assured of each other's love without taking it for granted.

＊

Love is no assignment for cowards.
OVID

＊

I promise to devote my energy to care for you, our families, and the bond that grows between us.

＊

Happiness belongs to the self-sufficient.
ARISTOTLE

＊

I vow to tell you the truth always, about both my fears and my feelings, so that minor worries will never become major dramas.

Action may not always bring happiness, but there
is no happiness without action.
BENJAMIN DISRAELI

❋

As the man in your life, I vow be your hunter, gatherer,
protector, lover, confidante, and friend—just don't ask
me my opinion on your new clothes!

❋

When you are scared, I will steady you.
When you are anxious, I will calm you.
When you are proud, I will praise you.
When you are upset, I will listen.

❋

Above all, let our marriage be built on trust and honesty.
With that, everything else will fall into place.

❋

I give you my hand today. Hold it always.

When we feel love and kindness towards others, it not
only makes others feel loved and cared for, but it helps us
also to develop inner happiness and peace.

THE DALAI LAMA

＊

Let us vow today to say what we mean and mean what
we say. Empty words ring hollow.

＊

We mutually pledge to each other our lives, our fortunes,
and our sacred honor.

THOMAS JEFFERSON

＊

A pledge is easy to make and even easier to break. May
we never stop trying to live up to our promises today.

＊

I promise to share and discuss with you all
my thoughts and feelings, so that there is never any
room for doubt or confusion.

Marriage is built on many high principles,
love being principal of all.

※

There is a time for everything, and a season for
everything under heaven:
a time to search and a time to give up,
a time to keep and a time to throw away,
a time to tear and a time to mend,
a time to be silent and a time to speak.
ECCLESIASTES 3:1–7, THE BIBLE

※

May we grow more selfless every day.
Love looks not with the eyes but with the mind
And therefore is winged Cupid painted blind.
WILLIAM SHAKESPEARE

※

A good sense of humor can distract from many flaws.

It is not so much our friends' help that helps us,
as the confidence of their help.
EPICURUS

✳

We have e-mail, voicemail, cell phones, and
beepers, yet the simple squeeze of your hand tells
me all I need to know.

✳

Love is a thing as free as any spirit. Women naturally
desire liberty and not to be constrained like slaves.
And so do men, if I shall tell the truth.
GEOFFREY CHAUCER

✳

Who would give a law to lovers?
Love is unto itself a higher law.
BOETHIUS

Why do I love you? Because I don't have to say
a word and yet you understand. You are tuned in to me,
you are on my wavelength.

✳

Together we will share our love with the world. Together
our love will grow into a bond too strong to break.
FROM A SELECTION OF VOWS AT WWW.BWEDD.COM

✳

When a match has equal partners, then I fear not.
AESCHYLUS

✳

The little unremembered acts of kindness and love
are the best parts of a person's life.
WILLIAM WORDSWORTH

✳

You are everything I need and at this moment,
I know that all my prayers have been answered and
that all of my dreams have come true.
FROM A SELECTION OF VOWS AT WWW.BWEDD.COM